Breed Lover's Guide™

GERMAN SHORTHAIRED POINTER

A Practical Guide for the
German Shorthaired Pointer Lover

Tammy Gagne

German Shorthaired Pointer

Project Team
Editor: Stephanie Fornino, Mary E. Grangeia
Indexer: Dianne L. Schneider
Book Design: Mary Ann Kahn
Designer: Angela Stanford

T.F.H. Publications
President/CEO: Glen S. Axelrod
Executive Vice President: Mark E. Johnson
Publisher: Christopher T. Reggio
Production Manager: Kathy Bontz

T.F.H. Publications, Inc.
One TFH Plaza
Third and Union Avenues
Neptune City, NJ 07753

Printed and bound in China
11 12 13 14 15 16 1 3 5 7 9 8 6 4 2

Library of Congress Cataloging-in-Publication Data
Gagne, Tammy.
  German shorthaired pointer / Tammy Gagne.
      p. cm.
  Includes bibliographical references and index.
  ISBN 978-0-7938-4180-6 (alk. paper)
  1. German shorthaired pointer. I. Title.
  SF429.G4G34 2011
  636.752'5--dc22
                                 2010005240

This book has been published with the intent to provide accurate and authoritative information in regard to the subject matter within. While every reasonable precaution has been taken in preparation of this book, the author and publisher expressly disclaim responsibility for any errors, omissions, or adverse effects arising from the use or application of the information contained herein. The techniques and suggestions are used at the reader's discretion and are not to be considered a substitute for veterinary care. If you suspect a medical problem consult your veterinarian.

Note: In the interest of concise writing, "he" is used when referring to puppies and dogs unless the text is specifically referring to females or males. "She" is used when referring to people. However, the information contained herein is equally applicable to both sexes.

The Leader In Responsible Animal Care For Over 50 Years!®
www.tfh.com

CENTRAL
Garden & Pet

Table of Contents

4 Chapter 1: History of the German Shorthaired Pointer
The GSP in Germany, The GSP in England, The GSP in the United States

10 Chapter 2: Characteristics of Your German Shorthaired Pointer
Physical Characteristics, Living With Your GSP

16 Chapter 3: Supplies for Your German Shorthaired Pointer
Collar, Leash, Food and Water Bowls, Crate, Bed, Safety
Gate, Grooming Supplies, Identification, Toys

34 Chapter 4: Feeding Your German Shorthaired Pointer
Nutrients, Commercial Foods, Noncommercial Foods,
Free Feeding Versus Scheduled Feeding, Obesity

50 Chapter 5: Grooming Your German Shorthaired Pointer
Grooming Supplies, Coat and Skin Care, Ear Care, Eye Care, Dental Care,
Nail Care

64 Chapter 6: Training Your German Shorthaired Pointer
Why Train Your GSP?, Positive Training, Socialization, Crate
Training, Housetraining, Basic Commands

82 Chapter 7: Solving Problems With Your German Shorthaired Pointer
Barking (Excessive), Chewing, Digging, House Soiling, Jumping Up,
Nipping and Biting

96 Chapter 8: Activities With Your German Shorthaired Pointer
Traveling With Your GSP, Sports and Activities

112 Chapter 9: Health of Your German Shorthaired Pointer
Finding a Vet, Annual Vet Visit, Vaccinations, Breed-Specific Illnesses,
General Illnesses, Complementary Therapies, Senior GSPs

134 Resources

138 Index

History of the German Shorthaired Pointer

W henever I think of the German Shorthaired Pointer (GSP), I am reminded of a pair of these striking animals I met one Independence Day on a college campus on the coast of Maine. My family and I had arrived early to secure a good spot for viewing the annual fireworks display that would be launched from Portland's Eastern Promenade when I noticed them. One GSP was almost entirely brown, or liver, as I later learned the color was called. The other was a dazzling combination of liver and white ticking. It was impossible to decide which animal was more beautiful.

My first thought was to worry about what the dog's reactions would be when the colorful and extremely noisy show began once the hot July sun slipped into the Atlantic. Though fully grown, neither dog looked very old, and I knew that thunderous noise of this kind had been the ruin of many other young dogs each year on our country's birthday. "Oh, if there's one thing they're used to," their proud owner assured me, "it's loud noises. They're both hunting dogs." He went on to tell me more about them as they stood faithfully by his side, seeming to swell with dignity as he spoke about them.

The man and his dogs continued moving through the crowd to find their own grassy vantage point, stopping frequently to chat with other dog fanciers like me. I had all but forgotten them in the excited commotion of the evening

German Shorthaired Pointers have calm, confident temperaments.

BEST IN SHOW

*W*hat led to the first Best in Show title for a German Shorthaired Pointer at Westminster? No one can explain it better than Len Casey, the AKC judge who awarded Ch. Grethenhof Columbia River (aka Traveler) with this history-making win. Following the 1974 event, Casey told *Sports Illustrated*, "He was the first one who caught my eye. You can't fault the dog. He's as fine an example of a sporting dog as I've ever laid my hands on. That dog was in absolute full bloom. I'd love to get my 12-gauge out of the closet and go out in the field with him tomorrow." The second and only other GSP to win this prestigious title was Ch. Kan Points VJK Autumn Roses (aka Carlee). A direct descendant of Traveler, Carlee won the Best in Show title in 2005.

—until the show was over, that is. While maneuvering our way through the mass of people after the grand finale, I saw them once more. Both dogs were as relaxed and self-assured at the conclusion of the evening as they were when they arrived, and I strongly suspected that they had batted nary an eyelash at any time during the explosive performance.

The GSP in Germany

Were these German Shorthaired Pointers just incredibly well-trained dogs, or was their calm and confident temperament the result of decades of careful breeding? I suspected even then that the answer was a combination of the two. History certainly assures us that the German Shorthaired Pointer breed is indeed the result of painstaking planning.

In the United States the breed is called the German Shorthaired Pointer, but in its native Germany it is known simply as Kurzhaar, meaning shorthair. Although no one can say for certain, most people think that the GSP, as he is commonly known, descended from the German Bird Dog. It is likely, however, that German scenthounds and track and trail dogs also contributed to this unique breed in the way of crossings. One might even say that the breed has Spanish roots, as the old Spanish Pointer was behind the German Bird Dog. It wasn't until the Germans crossed the GSP with the English Pointer, though, that the breed evolved into the versatile mix of athleticism, beauty, and sound temperament that it is today.

The first German Shorthaired Pointer was registered with the German Kennel Club in 1872. His name was Hektor I. In 1891 the

After decades of careful breeding, the GSP evolved into the versatile mix of athleticism, beauty, and sound temperament that he is today.

TIMELINE

- 1872: The first German Shorthaired Pointer was registered with the German Kennel Club.
- 1891: The Klub Kurzhaar was formed in Germany.
- 1930: The German Shorthaired Pointer was accepted by the American Kennel Club.
- 1941: The German Shorthaired Pointer Club of America sponsored its first specialty show.
- 1944: The German Shorthaired Pointer Club of America held its first field trial.
- 1951: The first German Shorthaired Pointer was registered in England.
- 1974: Ch. Grethenhof Columbia River became the first German Shorthaired Pointer to win Westminster's Best in Show title.
- 2005: Ch. Kan Points VJK Autumn Roses became the second German Shorthaired Pointer to win Westminster's Best in Show title.

WHAT IS A BREED CLUB?

Abreed club is a nonprofit organization of dog fanciers dedicated to the betterment of a particular breed. Many members are breeders and some do volunteer rescue work, but nearly all are owners just like you. Breed clubs often host specialty dog shows, providing owners a chance to enter these conformation events and also learn more about their favorite breed. One of the biggest responsibilities a breed club assumes is the crafting of the breed standard, which is used by the national kennel club in judging the particular breed in group or all-breed conformation events. Just as each country typically has its own kennel club, nearly all countries also have at least one breed club for each dog breed it recognizes.

first German Shorthaired Pointer club, the Klub Kurzhaar, was formed in Germany. It didn't take long for the breed's popularity to spread to other parts of Europe.

The GSP in England

The GSP was first exhibited in England in 1887 at the Barn Elms Show, but it was still many years before the breed was truly popular there. This was likely due to the country's fondness for hunting on horseback, something that required a canine companion with greater range and speed than the GSP offered. The first German Shorthaired Pointer was finally registered in England in 1951.

The GSP in the United States

Americans were quicker to welcome the German Shorthaired Pointer to their shores. The first German Shorthaired Pointer—a dog named Grief v.d. Fliegerhalde—was admitted to the AKC studbook in 1930. The first German Shorthaired Pointer specialty show sponsored by the American Kennel Club (AKC) followed in Chicago, Illinois, in 1941, with field trials beginning in 1944.

It was still some time before a German Shorthaired Pointer won a Best in Show title at the prestigious Westminster Dog Show in New York City, but the milestone event finally occurred in 1974, when a dog named Ch. Grethenhof Columbia River seized the title. In 2005 the second (and only GSP since) repeated this esteemed accomplishment. Her name was Ch. Kan Points VJK Autumn Roses. Today the German Shorthaired Pointer is among the 20 most popular breeds in the United States.

Characteristics of Your German Shorthaired Pointer

The German Shorthaired Pointer is a highly versatile dog breed. Combining the qualities of hounds and pointing breeds, the GSP can be used as a pointing dog, a tracking dog, or a retrieving dog. The breed can work in any terrain, including water. Some German Shorthaired Pointers are even used as sled dogs. What is even more impressive, though, is the GSP's can-do attitude. His focus and devotion make him, above all else, a faithful companion to be cherished for his incredible spirit.

Physical Characteristics

What most people notice first about the German Shorthaired Pointer is the breed's striking coloration.

Coat Color

Although some GSPs are a solid brown (called liver), most are a combination of liver and white. Some are liver dogs ticked with white, while others are liver

The German Shorthaired Pointer is a medium-sized dog.

patched with white ticking through the brown, and a few are called liver roans. These dogs have both brown and white hairs intermingled with each other, creating an especially eye-catching variegated appearance.

Ask the Expert

HUNTING DOG *AND* HOUSE PET

Are hunting dogs too lively to make good house pets?
Blaine Carter is a German Shorthaired Pointer breeder from Brunswick, Maine. As he told the *Portland Press Herald,* "The strength of the field experience quiets them in the house. They're calm in the house but energetic in the field—they just come alive in the field."

Puppy Love

PLEASED TO MEET YOU!

Introduce your German Shorthaired Pointer puppy to as many people as possible as soon as you bring him home. If you are worried about taking him out in public because he hasn't had all of his vaccinations yet, invite your family and friends (and their pets) to come to him. The best way to maintain your GSP pup's sweet temperament is by socializing him to both people and other animals from day one. If you put off this important training step, he may become a little standoffish as an adult when it comes to meeting new people. A GSP puppy, on the other hand, will approach socialization the way he does everything else: with utter exuberance.

Coat
The coat is short and feels rough to the touch due to its thickness. It is much softer and also sparser on the dog's head and ears.

Size
A medium-sized dog, the German Shorthaired Pointer stands approximately 2 feet (0.5 m) tall. Males typically measure between 23 and 25 inches (59 and 64 cm), with females falling between 21 and 23 inches (54 and 59 cm). If you plan to show your GSP in conformation events, his height should fall as close to these measurements as possible. Just 1 inch (2.5 cm) above or below is considered a serious fault. Male German Shorthaired Pointers weigh between 55 and 70 pounds (25 and 31.5 kg). Because females have a slightly smaller frame,

they usually weigh between 45 and 60 pounds (21 and 27 kg). Like the German Shorthaired Pointer's body, his neck and shoulders are muscular. Despite the dog's strapping appearance, his entire body is well proportioned.

Ears
The German Shorthaired Pointer's ears are also a fundamental part of the breed's trademark look. Long and broad, they lie close to the head, giving even an adult GSP the look of a playful pup at times.

Eyes
The almond-shaped eyes are, like the dog's nose, brown.

Muzzle
The muzzle is long and relatively broad, making it easier for the breed to seize game in the field.

Tail

At the end of the dog's short but powerful back is his tail. The tail is docked to 40 percent of its original length to prevent it from getting caught in the brush while hunting.

Legs

The legs are also strong and well muscled.

Living With Your GSP

Although the German Shorthaired Pointer is a hyper breed, it can be surprisingly easy to live with one of these dogs. They truly want to learn, so the secret to successful ownership is utilizing that high energy level in training.

The GSP gets along well with other animals, including other dogs.

Companionability With People

The German Shorthaired Pointer makes a wonderful family pet for the right family. This even-tempered dog is both smart and loyal. He enjoys meeting new people but can be a bit reserved around strangers if he isn't properly socialized. The GSP can also be protective of his loved ones. It is in his nature to want to please his owner, making the breed highly adaptable to a number of types of living situations. This quality also makes him very good at this work if his owner utilizes his abilities in the field.

Companionability With Other Animals

The breed gets along well with other animals, including fellow dog breeds and cats. Many breeders in fact feel strongly that German Shorthaired Pointers need the companionship of fellow canines—a pack, if you will—to be truly happy. Because the breed has a strong hunting instinct, though, pet birds and other small animals may be bad choices. What is most important is that your German Shorthaired Pointer is socialized properly so that he readily accepts new people and animals.

Environment

German Shorthaired Pointers can live virtually anywhere, as long as they have enough space. This is not a breed for

CHARACTERISTICS CHECKLIST

The German Shorthaired Pointer:
- ✓ is a highly versatile dog breed
- ✓ may be either solid liver or a combination of liver and white
- ✓ is known for his long ears
- ✓ has an athletic, muscular body
- ✓ can make an excellent pet for the right family
- ✓ values both his human and canine family
- ✓ must get regular exercise
- ✓ needs training and will get into mischief if left alone too long

apartment living and should never spend all day in a crate or kennel. Because GSPs are natural athletes, they need big yards and active family members with time enough to play with them.

Exercise

A simple stroll around the neighborhood is not enough exercise for this energetic animal. If you do not have a large fenced yard, you must get out with your German Shorthaired Pointer for a daily jog or twice-daily brisk walk. Swimming is also a fun and practical way for your GSP to get his exercise. Also, the fence enclosing a GSP's yard must be high, at least 6 feet (2 m). If left unsupervised, this breed can become an incredibly crafty escape artist.

Trainability

Because German Shorthaired Pointers are so intelligent, they are highly trainable.

Even if you never plan to hunt with your GSP, teaching him basic obedience is a good idea for many reasons. Most importantly, this breed needs something to do to be happy. When your GSP knows what you expect from him, it is easier for him to fulfill those expectations. Training can also be a great deal of fun for both you and your German Shorthaired Pointer. GSPs do not necessarily need to hunt, but they do need a purpose. If left to their own devices, they will come up with projects of their own, inevitably mischievous ones.

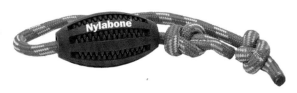

Chapter 3

Supplies for Your German Shorthaired Pointer

alking through the aisles of a pet supply store can be intimidating for a new dog owner. There are so many choices for the things your German Shorthaired Pointer needs—and so many others things that you wonder whether he needs at all. Heck, just choosing a store can be overwhelming, with so many local shops and national pet supply depots popping up everywhere these days. You can even buy your dog's supplies online from numerous retailers. Your best resource is a well-planned list. As far as the suppliers go, select one that you think will suit your shopping style the best. If you don't like it, try another the next time you need to buy

something for your GSP. Most stores offer the same basic products, and "basic" is the key word.

Begin by purchasing the basic supplies that your German Shorthaired Pointer truly needs. You can make note of any other things that catch your eye and postpone making decisions on those until after you have gotten all of the must-have items. I have found that many trendy pet care items go unused. They may seem like a good idea in the store, but their usefulness is often overestimated. The ones that will be really useful will continue to jump out at you when you return to purchase more food for your pet. Buying one or two superfluous things is okay, but you mustn't sacrifice an item your GSP needs for one that will be tossed in a donation box in a month's time.

Collar

The first thing you will need for your German Shorthaired Pointer is a well-fitting collar. You will need this item when you take your GSP home.

Collar Fit

To find your dog's collar size, place a measuring tape around his neck. The tape should be snug but not tight; you should be able to slip two fingers underneath it comfortably. If your dog is still a puppy, wait to buy his first collar until just a few days before his homecoming, and double-

The first thing you will need for your GSP is a well-fitting collar.

check with your breeder to make sure that your dog's neck hasn't grown since the initial measurement was taken. If you are adopting an adult dog, you may measure your new pet at any time and purchase a collar before taking him home. Some shelters even sell collars as a means of raising extra money.

Collar Types

When you visit your local pet supply store, you will see the numerous types of collars available for dogs. The three most popular materials are leather, cotton, and nylon.

Leather

Leather wears best but is the most expensive option. For this reason, you may consider cotton or nylon until your dog reaches his adult size at approximately six months of age. Once your dog is fully grown, though, investing in a leather collar is a smart step. Unlike cotton or nylon, leather won't ravel or fray over time.

Cotton

Cotton collars come in a variety of colors and prints, making them very pleasing to the eye. Another advantage to cotton is that it is extremely comfortable for your pet. I think of a cotton collar as being the canine equivalent of a human's favorite T-shirt. And like the classic white tee that I buy each season, a cotton collar will

Buckle collars are a popular choice among dog owners.

probably need to be replaced more often than either nylon or leather.

Nylon

Nylon collars are another popular choice among dog owners, and for good reason. This man-made material wears well and is usually the least expensive option. Also, like cotton, nylon is available in a wide range of colors and prints.

Slip

If your German Shorthaired Pointer is still learning to walk on a leash, you may wonder whether you should use a slip collar, also known as a choke collar or choke chain. This collar is essentially a length of rope or chain designed to tighten around your dog's neck when he pulls. The purpose of a slip collar is to teach a dog that when he pulls, he chokes himself. With proper and consistent

Ask the Expert

PUPPY PREP

*O*nce I have all of the necessary supplies, what should I do to prepare for my German Shorthaired Pointer puppy's homecoming?

German Shorthaired Pointer Club of America member Karen Detterich has been breeding GSPs since 1979. She shared with me, "Besides having the usual food, bedding, and pet care supplies ready for your GSP, your home should be prepared as if a busy toddler were due to arrive. Remove the temptation of nondoggy items from your puppy's reach. Your puppy should want to be in your company while in the house. If he wanders out of sight, he is probably up to some trouble. Close doors or use barriers to keep the puppy near you, and have a cage or safe, penned area for him when he cannot be attended to."

training, a slip collar should not be necessary for your GSP.

Martingale, Head Harness

If your dog is an adamant puller, I recommend using a martingale collar or a head harness. A martingale collar looks like a conventional dog collar, but it will tighten slightly when a dog pulls as a gentle reminder that pulling only hinders him from getting where he wants to be. The most important difference between a slip collar and a martingale is the limited constriction of the latter item; the martingale is much safer for your pet. A head harness fits over a dog's snout and clasps behind the head. It discourages pulling by bringing the dog's head downward when he pulls. When a dog cannot see where he is going, he won't pull.

Prong

Prong collars, or pinch collars, should never be used on a GSP. As the name implies, this metal collar contains tines that push into a dog's neck if he pulls while wearing it. Like the martingale, a prong collar does limit the amount of constriction applied to a dog's neck. Unlike the martingale, however, the potential for injury from a prong collar is high. If your dog's pulling problem is severe enough that you are considering using one of these extreme training tools, your dog may likely pull to the point of injury. No dog should ever suffer a laceration as a result of a pulling habit. If you are at the end of your proverbial rope when it comes to your dog's pulling, contact a professional trainer.

A short leash is ideal for trips to your dog's potty spot, neighborhood walks, and veterinary checkups.

When to Wear the Collar

Your dog should always wear his collar when he is outside or in a public place. The tags on your dog's collar will help identify your pet should he ever become lost. Even in a fenced dog park or other secure area, collars are important. It is much easier to leash your dog when you are ready to leave or if a scuffle arises if he is wearing his collar.

If your GSP will be wearing his collar all the time, a collar with breakaway technology is best. This special type of collar is designed to break apart to prevent strangulation if it gets caught on something. When attaching your dog's leash, be sure to hook it through both of the metal loops. If you attach the lead to only one loop, a breakaway collar will come apart if your dog pulls too hard. Most breakaway collars are made of nylon. While nylon isn't quite as durable as leather, it will still wear quite well. Safety is most important and should always come first.

Leash

Once your German Shorthaired Pointer has a collar, you will need a leash to attach to it for walks and other outings. I recommend having at least two different leashes for your GSP. A short leash (between 4 and 6 feet [1 and 2m] long) is ideal for trips to your dog's potty spot, neighborhood walks, and veterinary checkups. A longer leash can be useful for walking your dog in open spaces. It also will come in handy when training your pet.

Leather, Cotton, and Nylon

Like collars, dog leashes come in a wide variety of styles made from various materials. Again, leather is usually the most practical choice for reasons of durability, but cotton and nylon have their advantages too. You should never allow your puppy to chew his leash, but while your dog is still learning this rule, you may want to use a less expensive material to keep costs down.

Chain

You can also find leashes made of chain. The biggest advantage of chain is that it is even hardier than leather. The foremost downfall of chain is its heavier weight. A chain lead can feel burdensome on your hand and heavier than necessary on even a muscular dog's neck.

Retractable

Retractable leashes have become amazingly popular in recent years. These adjustable-length leads are housed in plastic cases, many with ergonomic handles to make holding them more comfortable. Owners can limit their dogs to just a few feet (m) or give their pets as many as 30 feet (9 m) of freedom when appropriate.

You must be cautious when walking your dog on a retractable leash in high-traffic areas, even at shorter lengths. If the dog becomes tangled in the line, the recoil feature will temporarily become disengaged, and you may not be able to reel him in before he is placed in a dangerous situation. You also must make a point of inspecting the cord periodically to make sure that it has not become frayed. It can be easy to overlook any worn spots because this type of lead spends most of its time within its case.

Most importantly, make sure that the model you choose is made for a dog the size of your GSP. A model intended for a lighter-weight animal could snap if used with a larger dog. If you buy a retractable leash, read and follow all of the directions carefully. And remember, no dog should ever be allowed to run at full speed to the end of the line.

Having an adjustable leash is a lot like having multiple leads in one. Even if you buy a retractable lead, however, it is smart to purchase at least one conventional leash as well. Using a specific leash for potty training can help your dog distinguish between walks for pleasure and those intended for the purpose of elimination.

Food and Water Bowls

The next thing your German Shorthaired Pointer will need is a pair of bowls: one for food and one for water. Your choices for your dog dishes are almost as abundant as the assortment of collars and leashes available at most pet supply stores. Like those other necessities, though, some options are better than others. Be sure that the bowls you select are big enough for your dog. An adult GSP will eat somewhere between two and five cups of food each day. Don't forget to pick up some of the food your dog has been eating. Whether you plan to keep him on this particular regimen or not, you will need at least some of this food. Dietary changes should always be made gradually, mixing your dog's old food in a decreasing ratio with his new food. Doing this will help to keep your dog from experiencing stomach upset during the transition.

No matter what type of bowls you choose—stainless steel, ceramic, or plastic—I recommend purchasing two sets. That will make it easier to always have a clean set of dishes available for your dog. Both your dog's food and water bowl should be washed daily to prevent germs and other harmful organisms from growing.

Stainless Steel

Stainless steel is the best choice by leaps and bounds. In addition to being economical, stainless steel won't break, even if your dog kicks his bowl across the floor. Some German Shorthaired Pointers have been known to do this on purpose, but an even greater number do it occasionally by accident. Stainless steel is also very easy to clean. Just use regular dish soap or pop your dog's dishes into your dishwasher—no pesky top-shelf-only rules need apply. Perhaps most importantly, though, a stainless

Your GSP will need a pair of bowls: one for food and one for water.

bowl will have no negative effects on your dog's health.

Ceramic

Ceramic pet dishes, while very pretty, can contain lead, a highly toxic metal. By law, tableware for people cannot contain lead, but similar regulations protecting our pets from the lead have not been passed, even though exposure to high levels of lead can cause damage to an animal's brain, nervous system, liver, and kidneys. If you must buy ceramic bowls for your GSP, skip the trip to your pet supply store. Instead, buy only high-fire or table-quality items intended for human use from a reputable department store or kitchen

Plastic pet dishes, while convenient, can harbor bacteria and so are not an ideal choice for your GSP.

supply retailer. But remember, even lead-free ceramic bowls will break if dropped.

Plastic

Plastic may seem like a reasonable material for pet dishes. It's inexpensive and won't break if you drop it. Unfortunately, this is where the list of advantages of plastic ends. The hot water used by dishwashers is ideal for killing germs, but it can melt certain types of plastic. The biggest reason not to choose plastic bowls for your dog is safety. Eating and drinking from plastic dishes can cause your dog to develop plastic dish dermatitis. Triggered by a reaction to an antioxidant in the plastic, this common condition can lead to a loss of pigment in your dog's nose and lips. The color may or may not return when use of the plastic dishes is discontinued. Even more importantly, this contact dermatitis can cause pain and inflammation.

Crate

Buying your German Shorthaired Pointer a crate, or kennel, will make life easier for both you and your dog in many ways. First, a crate is a safe place for your puppy to hang out whenever you cannot supervise him. Crates limit a dog's opportunities for inappropriate chewing and other destructive behaviors. They

Puppy Love

LITTLE TEETH CAN BECOME BIG PROBLEMS WITHOUT TOYS

You may have to wait to purchase certain items for your German Shorthaired Pointer until he is fully grown and trained. An expensive dog bed, for example, may be wasted on a pup who is still in the midst of housetraining and teething. Buying toys for your precious pet, however, must never be postponed. Certainly you may limit your purchases to just a couple of toys at a time while your dog is still teething, but the mere fact that he is teething is the very reason he needs something safe to put in his mouth. If you do not provide your GSP pup with adequate playthings during this period, the chances of his destroying your belongings are much greater. Having toys also helps reduce boredom, a precursor to many problem behaviors. Start your German Shorthaired Pointer out on the right paw by occupying both his teeth and his time.

can also protect your dog from getting hurt or running out the door. Second, a crate will help you housetrain your new pet. Dogs tend not to soil the areas in which they rest. Using a crate drastically limits the number of housetraining accidents you will have to clean up. Simultaneously, it increases the odds for your dog to eliminate in the proper spot, setting him up for success in this area.

Owning a crate is a lot like having a multipurpose room for your dog. The crate can be an ideal dining room for your GSP, especially if you own other pets and want to keep their food separate. It can also serve as a bedroom (for naps or overnight), a playroom for enjoying chew toys, and even a quiet refuge. You will be amazed by how

often your dog seeks out his crate just because he feels like spending some time there.

Crate Types

Dog owners have two basic options when it comes to crates: plastic or wire. Each type offers its own advantages. Which kind of crate works best for your German Shorthaired Pointer depends on your individual dog's personality and your lifestyle. Because they are impractical, I advise against buying wooden or soft-sided crates. Both are extremely susceptible to damage from chewing, but the latter option just isn't sturdy enough to safely contain a large dog. A smaller pet might be able to chew his way out, but a larger dog like a German Shorthaired

Pointer could burst the seams with his strength alone.

Plastic

Plastic crates are the preferable choice for owners who plan to travel with their dogs. Most airlines require that dogs ride in noncollapsible crates, making plastic the more sensible option. A plastic crate is also a safe spot for your dog when riding in your vehicle, and foldaway models are especially convenient for this type of travel. Plastic also has its disadvantages. Although most plastic crates have vented sides for proper air circulation, visibility may be low. If your GSP values privacy, the limited view may not be a problem for him. If, on the other hand, he is a social butterfly, he may feel estranged from the rest of the family when spending time in his crate. Plastic can also be a poor choice for chewers.

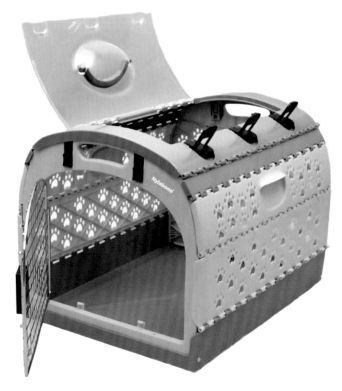

Be sure to select a crate that is the proper size for your GSP.

Wire

A wire crate allows a dog plenty of interaction with other household members, depending on where you place it, of course. If more privacy is needed, owners can always place a towel or blanket over one side. Because most wire crates are collapsible, they can be stored easily when not in use. Just be sure that someone in your household isn't intimidated by this daunting phrase: some assembly required.

Crate Size

Be sure to select a crate that is the proper size for your GSP. Each manufacturer uses its own classifications, but you will probably want a large model—approximately 42 inches (106.5 cm) long. Your dog should be able to stand, turn around, and lie down comfortably inside his crate. If the crate is too small, he won't enjoy spending time in it. Avoid going with a crate that is even a little too big, though, or your dog may be tempted to use one end as a bathroom. If this happens, it can ruin the crate's potential as a housetraining tool.

While your German Shorthaired Pointer is still a puppy, block off the superfluous space in his crate to discourage him from soiling this area. A cardboard box works well for this purpose. This partition can be removed once your dog has reached his full size.

Crate Liner

Finally, don't forget to purchase at least one crate liner. A liner should match the dimensions of the crate's floor and be at least a couple of inches (cm) thick. It should also be machine washable, as it will get dirty from time to time. I recommend buying two liners if you can so that you always have a clean replacement on laundry day.

Bed

Every German Shorthaired Pointer needs a place to sleep. Perhaps you plan to crate train your new dog. If so, his kennel will also serve as his bed. If, on the other hand, you prefer a dog bed to a crate, you need to find a canine cot that your GSP will find more comfy than your own bed covers. Either way, it is extremely important that you select and purchase this item as early as possible. Allow your dog to spend just one night atop your own bed's cozy covers and—I assure you—you will be sleeping with insufficient leg room for many years to come.

When choosing a dog bed, select one that will be easy to clean. Look for a cover that can zip off and be tossed into the washing machine for easy laundering. (Some manufacturers even hide the zipper when closed to deter chewers.) Also, make sure that you know what is inside the bed. Beds filled with cedar shavings may be comfortable, but they can be rough on a sensitive nose—either your German Shorthaired Pointer's or your own. Better choices include memory foam, shredded foam, and hypoallergenic fiberfill.

If your GSP is still a puppy, you may want to postpone investing in a bed until your dog can be trusted not to chew or soil it. An old blanket or comforter can work well in the meantime. Just fold it a few times and place it where your dog's bed will go. A blanket can also serve as a temporary crate liner.

Safety Gate

If you do not plan to crate train your German Shorthaired Pointer, I highly recommend investing in a safety gate. Like a crate, a gate can be used to confine your pet when you cannot watch him properly. Unlike the crate, however, a gate can afford your pet the space of an entire puppy-proofed room.

Safety gates can be found at most pet supply stores or your local department store in the baby section. Some styles are portable and can be pressure mounted in any doorway; others can be more permanently installed to swing open and shut as needed in a specific part of your home. Be sure that the model you choose is high enough that your German Shorthaired Pointer cannot merely jump over it.

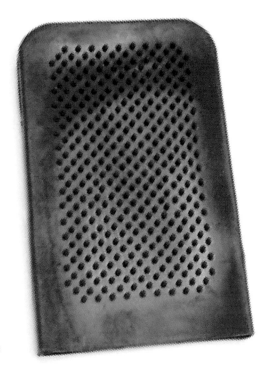

A grooming mitt is just one grooming supply you will need to purchase for your GSP.

Grooming Supplies

Grooming a German Shorthaired Pointer is not at all complicated or time consuming. It is important, however, that you buy the correct tools. These include a rubber horse brush or grooming glove, a toothbrush, and nail clippers. Because this breed's coat is so short, your pet's hair won't mat or tangle, but he will shed. With his contrasting light and dark coat, your GSP will leave visible hair on all colors of carpeting and clothing. You can minimize shedding tremendously, though, with regular brushing. Some owners opt to use damp gauze squares for brushing teeth, so you may be able to skip buying a toothbrush, but nail clippers will be an absolute necessity.

In addition to these tools, you will also need to purchase a few disposable items. Whether you go the gauze route or opt for a traditional toothbrush, you will need to purchase a tube of canine toothpaste. Never use human toothpaste on your dog, as it can make him sick. You won't need to bathe your German Shorthaired Pointer very often—only about once every month or two, but you will need some dog shampoo for when the time comes. Like toothpaste, human shampoo is not recommended for dogs because the pH of their skin differs dramatically from ours. Also, because of the shape and fold of the GSP's ears, moisture and bacteria can become trapped within them easily. For this reason, regular ear cleanings are a must for preventing infection. You can find ear cleanser, along with the other grooming supplies you will need, at your local pet supply store—or you can make your own ear-cleaning solution from equal parts of vinegar and water.

You must provide your dog with identification, whether it be ID tags or a microchip, or both.

Identification

When you register your dog with your local municipality, you will receive a numbered dog tag. When attached to your dog's collar, this item can help identify him if he ever becomes lost. To the average person on the street, however, this number alone means nothing. A better way to provide your dog with identification is to buy him a personalized tag.

Tags

Personalized tags are extremely inexpensive and easy to find. Many pet supply stores offer self-serve machines that engrave animal tags in just minutes while you wait. You can also order this custom-made item online. Be sure to include your dog's name, your address, and your phone number (including area code). And don't forget to attach the tag to your dog's collar. If he doesn't wear it, a tag is useless.

Microchips

The most permanent form of identification is a microchip. If your dog is ever stolen, a tag will do little to bring him back to you. Even a dimwitted thief will make it a top priority to remove your German Shorthaired Pointer's ID tag.

Microchipping your GSP is a much more permanent and effective choice. A canine microchip, which is approximately the size of a grain of rice, can be inserted under your dog's skin (typically between his shoulder blades) with a needle during a routine veterinary visit with absolutely no anesthesia. The process is no more painful than a vaccination. Your dog's unique number is then registered with the appropriate company. If your German Shorthaired Pointer becomes lost or stolen, a veterinarian or animal shelter worker can scan the chip to confirm his identity.

It is extremely important that you keep your contact information current with your microchip company. If you move or change your phone number, be sure to provide an update. Likewise, if you move far enough to switch to a different veterinarian, remember to let the new office staff know that your dog has been microchipped. Your dog's chart should include this important number.

The American Kennel Club (AKC) encourages owners to microchip their dogs. In certain areas, a microchip is even required by law if you own a dog. In 1995 the city of Oakland, California, became one of the first municipalities to draft an ordinance making it a crime not to microchip a canine companion.

As the practice of microchipping has become more and more popular, it has also become surprisingly affordable. Low-cost vaccination clinics, which are held at many pet supply stores, frequently offer

German Shorthaired Pointers enjoy playing with a variety of toys.

microchipping at a reduced cost for pet owners. This can be especially helpful if you own more than one animal.

Tattoos

At one time the most popular method of canine identification was tattooing. Many dog owners still go this route. Like a person's tattoo, a dog's tattoo is applied just under the animal's skin with a needle filled with special ink. Unlike a human being, though, a dog must be anesthetized during this procedure. Another downfall to this method is that a tattoo can be altered, rendering it far less useful than a microchip.

Toys

Most German Shorthaired Pointers love toys. The type your dog likes best will depend on his personality.

Types of Toys

Perhaps your GSP enjoys chasing balls or squeak toys. My female Cocker Spaniel, Molly, especially likes pigs and cows. Whenever we take her to the pet supply store, she will inevitably reach for one of these stuffed toys. Your dog might not be as specific in his likes and dislikes, but most do have preferences toward one type of toy or another.

Check It Out

SUPPLIES CHECKLIST

- ✓ properly fitted collar and leash
- ✓ food and water bowls (two sets are better than one!)
- ✓ crate and bedding
- ✓ safety gate
- ✓ rubber horse brush, soft-bristled brush, or grooming glove
- ✓ toothbrush (or gauze squares) and canine toothpaste
- ✓ nail clippers
- ✓ ear cleanser (or white vinegar to mix with water)
- ✓ identification tag
- ✓ toys, toys, and more toys!

If your dog is a chewer, reach for hardier items. Hard plastic toys work best for these German Shorthaired Pointers. Nylabone makes a fun line of toys for strong chewers. Molly also loves her Nylabone brontosaurus, a flavored chew toy shaped like a dinosaur.

Interactive toys are perfect for providing your pet with daily exercise. After all, any toy is more fun when a dog has someone to throw it for him. Try a flying disc for a fun workout for both you and your pet right in your own back yard.

Toys may also be found right on your kitchen counter. My own dogs regularly beg for empty paper towel tubes and plastic sodapop bottles. Think of the child at Christmas who has more fun playing with the paper than the presents. To my dogs getting a paper towel tube is a huge deal, probably because I only let them have this special treasure every once in a while. You see, the downside to this

makeshift toy is that it can make a big mess if your dog likes to shred it, as mine do. Picking up the pieces is more than worth it, though, when I see how much enjoyment this simple item offers them.

An empty soft drink bottle, on the other hand, makes no mess at all, but it can be extremely noisy when a dog chases it as it rolls across the floor. This is not an item to give your German Shorthaired Pointer if you have a headache. Also, be sure your dog doesn't puncture the plastic with his teeth or eat the cardboard from the paper towel tube. Both these items require owner supervision.

Beware of Vinyl Toys

Beware of vinyl toys. Toxic chemicals called phthalates are added to plastic to make it pliable. These chemicals also are what gives vinyl its characteristic smell. The stronger a toy made from vinyl smells, the more phthalates it likely contains.

The very property that makes phthalates so effective in softening plastic is the reason they are so dangerous: Phthalate molecules do not bond to the plastic but rather move freely through it—into any surface with which the plastic comes into contact, including your dog's skin and other tissue. They even release into the air, water, and earth.

In recent years there has been a great deal of scrutiny about vinyl toys made for children. Research has shown that these additives interfere with the proper development of young people. Many regional and national governments around the world have even passed legislation restricting the use of phthalates in childcare items. In 2007 Governor Arnold Schwarzenegger signed a bill that banned the use of phthalates in children's products in California. Perhaps most compelling, though, is that the bulk of the research on phthalates has been conducted on animals. Dogs in particular are extremely vulnerable to the effects of phthalates because their primary means of grasping an object is with their mouths.

Check the Label

Always check a toy's label before purchasing it. If you see the word "vinyl" or the initialization "PVC" (which stands for polyvinyl chloride), it means that the toy contains phthalates. If a toy isn't clearly labeled, keep looking until you find a suitable item that you are certain doesn't contain any of these harmful ingredients.

With increasing awareness of the dangers of phthalates, some companies have begun labeling their vinyl pet toys phthalate-free or nontoxic vinyl. Unfortunately, random testing of many products has determined that even toys bearing such claims do indeed contain these dangerous additives. There simply isn't such a thing as nontoxic vinyl. The only way to avoid phthalates is to avoid vinyl.

Chapter
4

Feeding Your German Shorthaired Pointer

K eeping your German Shorthaired Pointer healthy begins with selecting a nourishing feeding regimen for him. Fortunately, dog owners have many sound options when it comes to selecting foods for their pets in this day and age. Unfortunately, though, no one dog food formula is best for all dogs, not even for all members of a specific breed. Your GSP may thrive on a high-quality brand of kibble made from chicken, whereas another GSP may be allergic to chicken. For this dog, venison or fish may be a better protein source. Another dog may do best on a home-cooked feeding

Whatever food you choose for your GSP, make sure that it doesn't use meat by-products.

plan based on an entirely different main ingredient. The key to choosing the best diet for your pet is first to learn about nutrients that his body needs and second to observe how your dog reacts to the specific foods you give him.

Nutrients

Your German Shorthaired Pointer must eat a nutritious, balanced diet to stay healthy. He needs protein to aid in the growth and repair of body tissue, fat for energy and keeping him warm, and vitamins and minerals to boost his immune system and help his organs do their jobs. Although opinions differ as to the need for carbohydrates in the canine diet, carbs can offer your dog many benefits—including regulating his protein and fat metabolism. Just like human beings, though, dogs need a proper ratio of all of these nutrients to reap their many rewards.

Proteins—The Good, the Bad, and the By-Products

Protein should compose the biggest part of your dog's diet. The actual percentage should fall between 26 and 30 percent. A dog with a chronic condition such as an autoimmune disease or kidney problems should have less protein, however. Protein helps your GSP's body form enzymes and antibodies. Enzymes are important for proper digestion, and antibodies are vital for a strong immune system. Protein even

LIFE IS JUST A BOWL OF WATER

Water is one of the most important nutrients your German Shorthaired Pointer consumes each day. Staying properly hydrated is vital to all of his body functions. Water helps regulate your dog's body temperature, it carries nutrients throughout his body, and it helps to remove wastes from his system in the form of urine. Your GSP may need more water during warmer weather, after intense exercise, and while recovering from an illness. Dogs eating dry food also need to drink more water than those eating canned food, which contains a high proportion of water.

plays a fundamental role in the process of blood clotting.

The best sources for protein are lean meats and meat meal. At one time beef and chicken were the two basic protein choices for most dog owners, but you can now find foods made from lamb, turkey, various types of fish, and even bison at your local pet supply store. Which is best for your dog depends on his individual taste and needs.

Many owners have found that their dogs are allergic to beef or chicken. Even lamb, the quintessential hypoallergenic ingredient a decade or so ago, has begun to surface as a common food allergen for many dogs today, perhaps because it has been overused as an alternative protein source. Turkey can be a smarter choice than chicken because turkey is a relatively new dog food ingredient; therefore most dogs have not been

overexposed to it. Fish such as haddock, herring, and salmon are also excellent sources for protein. The omega-3 essential fatty acids in these types of fish help prevent cardiovascular disease, strengthen the immune system, and improve the look and feel of your German Shorthaired Pointer's coat. Omega-3s have even been shown to slow down the growth of cancer. Bison, an ingredient we are seeing on more and more dog food labels, is one of the leanest red meats and a wonderful protein source for dogs who enjoy beef.

What matters most is that the food you choose doesn't use meat by-products. These remnant parts of the animal may include beaks, necks, and feet—parts that are considered unfit for human consumption. Using by-products is cost effective for a dog food company that cares more about its bottom line than the health of its customers' pets, but

The proper diet will help keep your puppy happy and healthy.

eating by-products will do nothing for your dog's health.

Fats

Dogs generally need much more fat in their diets than people do. Whereas we tend to store fat, our dogs convert it into energy. Fats, or lipids, are an important energy source for your pet, especially if he is extremely active. Fats act as carriers for many important vitamins, including A, D, E, and K. These vitamins are classified as fat-soluble vitamins because excess amounts are stored in the fat within the body. Fats actually help your dog absorb vitamin D, making calcium more accessible within his body. Fats also help his body convert carotene into vitamin A.

Fats also make food taste good. The most nutritious dog food on the market cannot do your dog any good if he won't eat it. Beware of foods that are too high in fat, however. A food that contains more than 20 percent fat can cause your German Shorthaired Pointer to become overweight. If your dog is already too heavy, give him a food that is lower in fat until he has once again reached his ideal weight.

Carbohydrates—Should You Go With or Against the Grain?

Among the most common carbohydrate sources used in dog foods are grains. Whole grains in specific contain B-complex vitamins and vitamin E. Other popular canine carbohydrate sources include vegetables like corn, carrots, and sweet potatoes and fruits such as apples and blueberries. These foods contain a variety of vitamins that dogs need. Experts disagree as to the amount of carbohydrates a dog should eat. Many dog foods are made up of as much as 50 percent carbs. Others fall closer to the 15 percent mark. Some formulas contain virtually no carbohydrates whatsoever.

If you have been to a pet supply store recently, you have probably seen many dog food formulas labeled grain-free. One of the biggest reasons so many dog food companies have begun eliminating grains from their ingredient lists is that grains such as corn and wheat are among the most common canine allergens. Many manufacturers of low-quality dog foods use these grains as filler ingredients in their foods to keep their costs down. Not all grains are bad, however. Many whole grains like barley, brown rice, and oatmeal are highly digestible and contain vitamins, minerals, fats, and even proteins. Some of the nutrients found in whole grains cannot be obtained from meat-only diets.

Many dog owners believe that dogs do not need carbohydrates. Proponents of limiting (or eliminating) grains from dog foods often cite that wild dogs, after all, eat meat, not grains. While there is some truth to this assertion, an important piece of the picture is missing. The diets of wolves and other wild canines are indeed composed primarily of meats such as the carcasses of caribou, deer, elk, and rabbits. It's important to mention that when wild canines eat these animals, one of the first parts they consume is the intestines, which contain grasses, leaves, and other plants that the herbivores have consumed. Many people don't realize that wild canines also eat small amounts of grasses and berries directly.

A better goal is to limit your German Shorthaired Pointer's refined carbohydrate sources, which include white rice and white flour and contain virtually no vitamins, minerals, or fiber. The healthy parts of these ingredients have been stripped away prior to the manufacturing process. What is left is a source of calories and energy devoid of nutrients.

Vitamins and Minerals— Should You Supplement?

Your German Shorthaired Pointer needs a number of vitamins and minerals in his diet. These include various forms of vitamins A, B, D, E, and K. Your GSP will

AN IMPORTANT MILESTONE

Start transitioning your German Shorthaired Pointer puppy to an adult dog food formula between five and six months of age. Puppies need more protein in their diets than adult dogs, so as your dog reaches his adult size, his body will need less of this nutrient. Don't wait until you are at the bottom of the puppy food bag to make this change, though. Instead, gradually reduce the amount of puppy food you give your pet, replacing it with the adult formula. Begin by feeding 25 percent of the new food, moving to 50 percent the next week, and so on until your dog is completely transitioned. Selecting an adult food made from the same protein source as your GSP's puppy formula will also make him less likely to experience stomach upset as a result of the change. If you feed your GSP three meals a day, eliminate his midday meal around this time period. Continue to feed your dog the same amount of food, but divide it into two servings instead of three.

get vitamin A from foods rich in beta-carotene. Many of these foods (such as apricots, carrots, and sweet potatoes) sport a bright orange color, but beta-carotene is also found in spinach.

Some B-vitamins can also be found in many fruits and vegetables, but others are found in meat. One of the best sources for vitamin B12 and folic acid (another important B-vitamin) is organ meat. Your dog also needs vitamin D and calcium. Vitamin D is abundant in most dairy products, but because many dogs are lactose intolerant, fish is usually a better source for them.

Vitamin E is also found in fish, as well as in numerous vegetables, including beets, broccoli, carrots, pumpkin, and sweet potatoes. Vitamin K is found primarily in leafy green vegetables, such as kale and spinach.

The best sources of vitamins and minerals are the foods that contain these substances. If your dog is diagnosed with a medical condition, it may be wise to re-evaluate his diet in light of this discovery. Virtually every health problem can be better managed when optimum nutrition is part of the treatment plan. Some veterinarians even place patients on prescription diets designed for dogs suffering from particular diseases. Sometimes, however, what your dog's body needs cannot be procured from his food alone. Owners of older arthritic dogs, for example, may notice an improvement in their pets' mobility when they give them glucosamine supplements.

This natural compound is found in healthy cartilage.

Always consult your dog's veterinarian before giving your pet any type of supplement. Together you can decide what is best for your dog. If he does need a supplement, your vet will need to consider a variety of factors, such as your German Shorthaired Pointer's age and weight, when determining the proper dosage for him. Even natural supplements can be harmful under certain circumstances.

Commercial Foods

Commercial dog food has come a long way since its creation toward the end of the 19th century. Since that time, prepared dog foods have undergone several transformations. The first commercial dog food, which resembled a present-day dog biscuit, was called dog cake. In the 1930s canned dog food became all the rage, but the surge of this convenient prepackaged food was temporarily eclipsed by the commencement of World War II and the subsequent need for metals for the war effort. Dry dog food was introduced in the late 1950s. This early version of the kibble we know today became the staple of most dog-owning households of the 20th century. Still, these early foods were far from nutritious. Most were made with ingredients not considered fit for human consumption. This leads one to ponder whether the early commercial diets were better for dogs than the table scraps that had been fed to pets for centuries beforehand.

Today many pet food companies are rising to the challenge of creating a well-balanced diet for dogs. Numerous manufacturers offer formulas made with organic ingredients, a variety of vegetables and whole grains, and omega-3 fatty acids like flaxseed oil. Owners can find a healthy dog formula for nearly every purpose—from providing an active GSP with more energy to helping an overweight dog slim down.

Dry Food

Dry food remains the most popular choice of dog owners today. Unlike

Dry food remains the most popular choice of dog owners today.

wet dog food, kibble requires no refrigeration once opened. Owners can feed dry food whether their dogs eat their meals on a schedule or on a free-feeding routine. Perhaps the biggest reason owners prefer dry food is cost. Dry food is usually less expensive than canned or semi-moist formulas.

The biggest disadvantage to dry food is the amount of nutrients that are lost in the heat and pressure of the manufacturing process. Many vitamins, amino acids, and enzymes are destroyed during cooking and even during baking at high temperatures. As with most types of food, it's the processing that's the problem here. Some vitamins are added back into the foods before the bags are sealed, but I cannot stress it enough: Nutrients are best delivered directly from the foods your dog eats.

A great way to make sure that your German Shorthaired Pointer is getting a balanced diet is by supplementing his kibble with fresh vegetables and other healthy foods. You may do this daily or a few times a week. Adding a grated carrot or a few broccoli crowns to your dog's dinner is a nutritious way to make his food more appealing to him as well. Limit the amount of fruits because they tend to be high in sugar, and avoid onions altogether, as they cause anemia in dogs.

Adding a grated carrot to your dog's dinner is a great way to make his food more appealing to him.

Canned Food

While not as popular as kibble, canned dog food definitely has a strong following among pet owners. What I like best about canned food is that there is no need for preservatives. Because of its airtight design, a can of dog food doesn't require these additives to keep it fresh the way a bag of dry food does. Canned food is also more appealing to many pets because of its stronger aroma.

Canned food generally contains more protein and fat and less grain than kibble does. Whether this composition is a benefit or a liability depends largely on your individual dog's health and lifestyle. Canned dog food also contains far more water than dry food—as much as 75 percent of its total content. Because pound (kg) for pound (kg) canned food is more expensive than kibble, owners are paying more for canned food but getting less. Still, this added cost may be worth it if your GSP is a picky eater and the smell and flavor of canned food whet his appetite.

If an owner isn't meticulous about brushing a dog's teeth, wet food can wreak havoc on his oral health, especially if he eats canned grub exclusively. Soft wet food morphs into plaque and tartar amazingly quickly. If you feed your German Shorthaired Pointer canned dog food, you simply must make time for daily brushings.

If your older dog has loose or missing teeth from years of prior dental neglect, feeding wet food may be a kinder option than expecting him to try to chew kibble, but it is important that you also visit the vet. After a professional teeth cleaning, your dog's mouth will look, smell, feel, and be healthier.

Although wet foods aren't subjected to the same pressure during the cooking process, the effects from high heat are still factors with a canned diet. As with kibble, owners can supplement a canned diet with fresh vegetables and other healthy foods. The healthiest diets, after all, are the ones that include a variety of nutritious foods.

Semi-Moist Food

Semi-moist foods make up a smaller percentage of the dog food market. For a long time, most semi-moist foods contained excessive amounts of sugar, making these foods tasty but far from healthy. Like many other popular yet low-quality dog foods, these foods utilized artificial colors to make them look more appealing to the owners who purchased them. Some brands were even molded into the shape of burgers. Unlike real beef patties, however, these semi-moist burgers could be stored at room temperature in their individual packaging because of all the artificial preservatives they also contained.

HOME-COOKED TRANSITION

W*hat do I need to know before transitioning my German Shorthaired Pointer to a home-cooked feeding plan?*

Dr. Joy Lucas is a veterinarian at Upstate Animal Medical Center in Saratoga Springs, New York. As she told the *Times Union* newspaper, "We may have specific recommendations if we know a client is going to be switching to a home-cooked diet. You have to be committed to doing this home-cooked meal, and you have to be committed to not altering anything. You cannot alter anything in a given diet because that particular ratio has been evaluated and needs to be present in that form and in that ratio in order to make it completely balanced. You can't run out of eggs or forget to add a quarter teaspoon of salt."

Fortunately, semi-moist dog food has evolved into a much healthier middle ground between dry and wet food in recent years. The most popular semi-moist foods of today are dog food rolls. Packaged similar to salamis, dog food rolls are available in a wide variety of formulas. Some of the best names in canine nutrition offer diets in this medium.

Some owners feed this semi-moist food in addition to other dog foods; others feed it as a regimen of its own. I have found that this type of food also makes excellent high-value treats for training. Because this food is soft, it can also be a smart alternative to kibble for an older dog with dental problems. Like canned food, though, a semi-moist diet means more time spent brushing your German Shorthaired Pointer's teeth. Also like wet food, dog food rolls must be refrigerated once opened.

Noncommercial Foods

As veterinarians, breeders, and owners have learned more and more about canine nutrition, we have discovered that many of the same foods that help maintain human health also help in keeping our dogs healthy. A carefully chosen assortment of lean meats and vitamin-rich vegetables can offer your German Shorthaired Pointer everything his body needs, but they need not be packaged in a bag or can. They can be purchased from your local grocery store, butcher, or farmer's market—and prepared for your pet right at home.

Home-Cooked Diet—Just Like Mama Made

Many owners think that the best way to know exactly what their dogs are eating is to prepare their pet's meals themselves. When I was a teenager, my mother used to cook for our pet Poodle. This was during the 1980s, and many of my friends regarded this practice as rather eccentric. What my high school chums didn't realize, though, was that my mother was actually ahead of her time. Today it is far more common for dog owners to cook for their pets.

Although it may seem that it would be time consuming and expensive, cooking for your German Shorthaired Pointer really doesn't take a lot of time or money. If you already cook for your human family members, you may hardly notice a difference adding one more mouth to your weekly menus. Of course, your dog cannot have certain foods that the people in your household enjoy, but you may be surprised by just how many meals you already make that your dog can also eat. The biggest difference between your meals and your dog's is the lack of seasoning your dog's food will need. Hold the salt and other spices on his meals unless a trusted recipe for dogs tells you to use them.

If you decide to cook for your dog, research carefully and consult with your veterinarian.

The most important thing to bear in mind when choosing to cook for your dog is that you must do your homework. Start by telling your dog's veterinarian about your plans. Your vet may be able to suggest books about home cooking to make the endeavor easier for you and more nutritionally sound for your pet. Home cooking requires a serious commitment to learning exactly which nutrients your dog needs—and to providing them to your pet every day. It is vital to understand that home cooking does not mean merely scraping your table scraps into your dog's food bowl. Cooking for your pet means making his dietary needs as much a priority as the rest of the family's.

Although I do not feed my own dogs home-cooked fare exclusively, I do offer them regular servings of healthy meals I know they enjoy as a supplement to their dry food. I have even begun using less salt in the meals I make my family so that my dogs can share more of the foods I prepare for my human family members. I have always joked that my dogs eat better than I do; now I am finally catching up with them.

Raw Diet

Raw diets have been around for decades. Known by the acronym BARF (which stands for bones and raw food), this regimen is based on the fact that most foods retain even more of their nutrients when they are served uncooked. Proponents of raw feeding plans point out that domesticated dogs evolved from wolves, after all, and a wolf's diet consists exclusively of raw foods. Many raw-feeding owners also insist that their dogs' excellent health, shiny coats, and increased energy levels are all evidence that this type of diet is ideal.

Raw diets typically include a variety of raw foods, including beef, chicken, and eggs. Vegetables are also an important part of this feeding regimen, as are a limited number of fruits and carbohydrates. If your dog tolerates dairy, cheese can also be fed. Owners may choose to prepare raw foods for their pets personally (many foods must be chopped or ground before serving) or to purchase prepackaged raw meals that can be frozen.

If you are having trouble getting your German Shorthaired Pointer to eat his vegetables, try offering them before any meats. Lima beans will always pale in comparison to sirloin in your GSP's eyes. Also, be sure that your dog is hungry when you feed him.

Critics warn that the risks associated with feeding raw foods vastly outweigh the rewards. My own vet agrees. He has told me that while raw diets have some advantages, the problems he sees in dogs eating raw food are usually serious ones.

You may feed your GSP puppy two to three times a day.

Bones, for example, can be great for a dog's teeth, but they pose a significant choking hazard. They can also cause life-threatening intestinal obstructions. Bacteria such as *E. coli* and *Salmonella* are also very real dangers, even for a dog's seemingly cast-iron stomach. Raw meats can also contain harmful parasites. Even freezing the meat does not necessarily eliminate the presence of these microorganisms.

Free Feeding Versus Scheduled Feeding

You may feed your German Shorthaired Pointer puppy two to three times a day.

More important than how often you offer his meals, though, is that you establish a consistent feeding schedule for your new pet. Most GSP puppies will eat as much food as they are given, so leaving food available at all times (also called free feeding) can quickly lead to obesity.

Obesity

Because German Shorthaired Pointers love eating so much, obesity can quickly become a problem if owners don't keep a watchful eye on their dog's food intake. Serious illnesses such as diabetes, heart disease, and joint problems are the sad side effects to your dog's eating food too

Check It Out

FEEDING CHECKLIST

✓ If you feed your German Shorthaired Pointer a prepackaged diet, choose one with no by-products.

✓ Remember, dogs need more fat in their diets than people do.

✓ Grain-free diets work well for some dogs but not for others.

✓ Dogs need vitamins A, B, D, E, and K, and the best way to get them is from the food they eat.

✓ Brush your dog's teeth as often as possible, especially if he eats wet food.

✓ Talk to your veterinarian before placing your German Shorthaired Pointer on a home-coooked diet to make sure that you aren't overlooking any important nutrients.

✓ Raw diets offer certain advantages, but they can be risky. They have just as many critics as supporters.

✓ Avoid feeding too many treats or too much food in general, as these can lead your dog down to the road to obesity.

high in fat and calories. It is important to remember that even healthy foods must be served in moderation. If your dog is eating more calories than he is burning each day—whether they are coming from french fries or carrot sticks—he will gain weight. And like people, dogs tend to put weight on much more quickly than they can take it off.

If your GSP is overweight, talk to your veterinarian about the best approach to remedy the situation. The two most obvious means of lowering that number on the scale are diet and exercise. You may need to approach the latter strategy

carefully, though, if your dog is obese or if he already suffers from a health problem. Exercise can be a bit of a problem for a severely overweight animal. You must increase your pet's activity level to increase his metabolism, but the extra weight he is carrying places him at an increased risk of injury.

Make Changes Slowly

Changes should always be made slowly. First, your vet may recommend transitioning your pet to a weight-control diet. A smart strategy is to also add exercise to your German Shorthaired

Pointers's routine gradually. If your long-term goal is to run 1 mile (1.5 km) with your dog each day, for example, you may start by walking about half this distance for the first week. As your pet's tolerance increases, you may then lengthen the walk or pick up the pace a bit.

Follow Your Vet's Orders

Follow your vet's orders carefully, especially if your GSP suffers from a medical condition. Exercise should always be a positive addition to your pet's routine. It should never exacerbate a health problem.

In extreme situations of obesity, your veterinarian may suggest placing the dog on a prescription diet for weight loss. Even diet pills are now available for dogs. A canine drug called dirlotapide works much the same as a human appetite suppressant. Because it minimizes hunger and prevents your dog's body from absorbing fat, dirlotapide is very effective. Still, both prescription diets and diet pills should be used only in extreme cases and for short periods of time.

Exercise

As your dog begins losing his extra weight, movement should become easier for him and his endurance should increase as well. Still, continue to make changes slowly. If you think that your dog is ready for running, begin by walking, a

great warmup for even the fittest dog. You may then jog together for a short distance before returning to walking, a necessary cool-down period, toward the end of your workout.

Jogging is far from your only choice when it comes to increasing your German Shorthaired Pointer's exercise level. If you and your dog enjoy visiting the beach, make swimming a part of his exercise routine. Bringing a ball or flying disc for him to chase can make all of that movement even more fun for both you and your pet. Be creative. In the summer our dog Molly will jump through the sprinkler with our son in our backyard. My husband and I regularly bring both of our dogs to a set of public tennis courts close to our home. This enclosed area is perfect for playing fetch.

Owners can also include their dogs in their own exercise routines. Many German Shorthaired Pointers love running alongside their favorite humans while they rollerblade or bike. Our dogs enjoy chasing soccer balls with our son while he practices his all-time favorite sport. What the dog is doing is far less important than the movement itself. By making physical activity an ongoing priority, owners can help their dogs avoid the problems caused by obesity.

Chapter
5

Grooming Your German Shorthaired Pointer

rooming your German Shorthaired Pointer will be one of the easiest parts of caring for him. The necessary tasks are few, straightforward, and relatively easy to perform. Even better, they won't need to be done very often. You must, however, make time for regular grooming. By spending just a few minutes each day, you can keep your dog looking and feeling great.

much this breed sheds. The best way to minimize shedding is to brush your dog as frequently as possible. Daily brushings are ideal, but depending on the amount of hair your individual dog sheds, you may be able to brush him only about once a week.

It is a smart idea to brush your German Shorthaired Pointer puppy every day after bringing him home. Doing so will help acclimate him to the grooming

Grooming Supplies

You will need the following items to stay on top of your German Shorthaired Pointer's grooming needs:

- dog shampoo
- ear cleanser
- nail clippers
- rubber horse brush, curry brush, or grooming glove
- toothbrush and canine toothpaste

Coat and Skin Care

Taking care of your German Shorthaired Pointer's skin begins with keeping his coat in proper shape.

Brushing

New owners of German Shorthaired Pointers are often surprised by how

Taking care of your GSP's skin begins with keeping his coat in proper shape.

Ask the Expert

KEEPING THE TEETH HEALTHY

What is the most important thing I can do to keep my German Shorthaired Pointer's teeth healthy?

Make brushing a regular part of your grooming routine. If you acclimate your GSP to having his teeth brushed while he's young, he will tolerate it much better—and be much less likely to need a professional cleaning down the road. Dr. Paul Sova, Jr., of the Dog and Cat Hospital in Paterson, New Jersey, sees patients regularly for this procedure, which requires anesthesia. As he told the *Bergen Evening Record*, "I clean the animal's teeth and send the owner home with a dental-care package. They are very good at brushing their pet's teeth for the first few days, but they end up blowing it off. Owners don't like doing things with their pets that their pets don't like. But the bottom line is that, where practical, it's the most effective way to prevent tooth decay."

process and make future sessions easier for both of you. Likewise, daily brushings can help an adopted dog get used to the brushing routine.

In addition to removing dead hair, brushing also removes dirt and other debris from your GSP's coat. Without brushing, your dog's only means of removing this debris is licking the matter from his fur. While most dogs perform at least some self-grooming, regular brushing is a great way to lessen your pet's exposure to any toxic substances he may encounter. Brushing also brings out the natural oils in your pet's skin and helps distribute them through his coat.

German Shorthair Pointers who spend the bulk of their time outdoors often develop an undercoat during the fall and winter. This soft fur will shed out in the spring. During the colder months, though, you may need to use a soft bristle brush to reach your dog's skin when brushing him.

How to Brush
Beginning at your dog's head, work toward his tail down one side by brushing the hair against the direction of growth. When you are done, repeat this step on the opposite side. Be gentle, but do make sure that you are reaching your dog's skin. Once you have finished brushing against the hair's growth, switch to brushing in the direction of the hair's growth as you move back to your dog's head.

Brushing your dog's coat before bathing him will make the grooming process easier and more efficient.

Bathing

Always brush your dog prior to bathing him. For long-haired breeds, this important step helps prevent wet hair from tangling, but a thorough pre-bath brushing is also a smart step for short-haired dogs. Brushing your dog's coat before bathing him will make the bathing process easier and more efficient. Many GSP owners brush their dogs with a rubber curry brush or grooming glove during the bath. You may find this method to be even more effective at removing dead hair, dirt, and other debris before shampooing your pet.

To prepare for your GSP's bath, the first thing you should do is turn the heat up (or turn the air-conditioning down) shortly before bathing him. Once wet, he will feel chilled if the air temperature dips below 80°F (27°C), so you may need to adjust the thermostat even if you feel comfortable. Second, gather all of the necessary bathing supplies—including a large towel, a soft washcloth, your dog's shampoo and ear cleanser, and a handful of cotton balls. I also recommend keeping a towel for your personal use nearby. It will come in handy for wiping your hands between steps, and it can be a lifesaver if you end up getting shampoo in your eye. The worst time to realize you have forgotten something important is when your dog is standing in his bathwater.

How to Bathe

The best place to bathe your German Shorthaired Pointer is your bathtub. Begin by positioning a nonskid mat in the bottom of the tub. Be sure to secure the mat before you place your dog in the tub to prevent slipping. You may need to run a small amount of water to help the suction cups stick to the surface. Some owners like to fill the tub with water when bathing their dogs. I recommend a minimalist approach here. A full tub of water is not only a waste, but it also takes longer to drain while you are waiting to rinse your pet. If your German Shorthaired Pointer doesn't enjoy bathing, these extra few minutes will seem like an eternity for both of you. Instead, fill the tub with just enough lukewarm water to cover your German Shorthaired Pointer's feet.

Once your dog has stepped into the tub, place a single cotton ball in each of his ears. This will help keep soap and water out of the ear canal. Next, wet your washcloth with plain water and gently wash your dog's face. Refrain from using shampoo in this area to avoid getting it in his eyes. Using your shower's detachable spray nozzle, wet your dog's neck, body, and legs down. I like to adjust the water temperature at the beginning of a bath and use the nozzle's pressure lever to turn off the spray when I don't need it. I still double-check the temperature before rinsing, but I eliminate the extra time needed to completely reset the temperature. If

Regular grooming can become a bonding experience with your dog.

SHAKE, SHAKE, SHAKE

The easiest way to teach your GSP to shake the water from his coat after a bath is to simply wait for him to perform this natural behavior on his own and reward him with heartfelt praise. As soon as your dog begins to wiggle his shoulders in a shaking motion, say "Shake" so he will associate the action with the word. As soon as he finishes, say "Good shake!" or "Good boy!" You may also keep an edible reward handy to reinforce the behavior. The more you practice and reward your dog for his compliance, the more likely he will be to perform the task on command. He may even link the behavior of shaking to your holding the towel out for him, making the verbal command unnecessary.

you do not have a detachable nozzle on your shower, I recommend picking one up at your local hardware or home improvement store. You can use a cup for rinsing, but it won't work nearly as well as this simple and inexpensive attachment. Look for one with at least 5 feet (1.5 m) of hose for reaching your entire pet. The best sprayers offer multiple spray settings. Use a massaging setting for wetting your dog down and a harder jet spray for rinsing him.

The most important thing to remember about canine shampoo is that it doesn't create the same amount of suds as human shampoo does. A little dog shampoo also goes a long way. Bear this information in mind when you squeeze a small amount of your pet's shampoo onto your washcloth and rub it to create

a modest lather. I wash my dogs much the same way I did my son when he was a baby: chest, belly, back, and legs first; bottom and feet last.

Once you have shampooed your dog, drain the tub and check the temperature on the water from the spray nozzle before rinsing him. And speaking of babies, that old-fashioned trick for checking an infant's bath water with your elbow works well for dogs too, but I prefer to use the inside of my forearm because this area feels even more sensitive to me. Because residual soap can irritate the skin, rinse your dog until the water comes clear.

Once you are certain that you have rinsed all of the shampoo from your GSP's coat, be sure to remove the cotton from his ears. A good friend of mine took her Cocker Spaniel to see the veterinarian recently, complaining that the aging dog seemed to be having some trouble hearing. After a quick inspection, the vet told my friend that he was pretty sure he'd found the problem—she had inadvertently left the cotton balls in place after her dog's most recent ear cleaning.

Using the large towel, gently squeeze most of the water from your dog's coat before allowing him to step out of the tub. It can be helpful to teach your German Shorthaired Pointer to shake when you hold a towel up between you after his bath. If you don't teach this command, your dog will still shake—but it will likely be at the most inopportune moment. Until your GSP has learned the *shake* command (see sidebar "Shake, Shake, Shake"), keep that extra towel for you handy.

Some owners like to use a blow dryer on their pets after baths. Blow drying is a great way to prevent your dog from feeling chilled, but you must make sure that you don't burn him. Always adjust the heat setting to low, and be sure to hold the dryer at least 8 to 12 inches (20.5 to 30.5 cm) away from your GSP. I recommend keeping a hand between the dryer and your dog at all times as an added safety precaution. Allowing your dog to air-dry is also a completely acceptable choice, providing the temperature is warm enough. Either way, finish up with one more brushing to remove any leftover dead hair.

Puppy Love

GROOM EARLY AND OFTEN

Teaching your German Shorthaired Pointer puppy to stand for grooming while he is young will save you many struggles when he is an adult. Even if he isn't due for a brushing or nail clipping, pick him up and place him on a table (holding him safely, of course) to give him a quick once-over with a brush or handle his feet whenever you think of it. Doing this not only will help your GSP feel more comfortable with having his coat brushed or his paws touched during toenail trims but also will help him acclimate to being stacked (posed) for being judged in a dog show in the event that you plan to participate in conformation. Praise your puppy for complying with grooming, whether you are simply checking his eyes or doing something more intensive, like cleaning his ears. You may even decide to offer him an edible reward for good behavior. The more positive you make the grooming experience, the better your German Shorthaired Pointer will tolerate it. He may even come to enjoy it.

By keeping your dog's long ears clean and dry, you will lessen his chances of developing an ear problem.

Ear Care

Because your German Shorthaired Pointer's ears fold downward and lie flat, the airflow into his ear canal is severely limited. This creates a warm, moist environment—ideal conditions for the emergence of an ear infection. By keeping your dog's ears clean and dry, however, you can lessen your GSP's chances of suffering from a problem that must be treated with antibiotics from your veterinarian.

How to Care for the Ears

Begin every cleaning with a quick inspection of each ear. First, look inside the ear. The skin should be a light pinkish color. You may notice some brownish wax deep inside the ear, but a black tinge or discharge of any kind usually indicates a problem. Second, sniff the ear. If you notice a foul odor, particularly a yeasty smell, this may be a sign of an infection. If the ear is sensitive to being touched, discontinue the home cleaning at once and contact your vet. Cleaning an infected ear at home can make diagnosis more difficult and can also cause your pet pain.

If the ear appears healthy, begin by squirting some ear-cleaning solution into the ear canal. This step is usually the one that causes a dog to balk. Your GSP may shake his head and pull away from you. Although you mustn't allow him to run away, the shaking is actually a productive reaction, as it helps loosen dirt and wax within the ear. Next, use a cotton ball or pad to gently wipe the ear clean. Never use a cotton swab because it can injure your pet. The canine ear canal is L-shaped, making it nearly impossible for you to hurt your dog with the cotton.

You may use several pieces of cotton before it starts coming out clean, or you may need to use only a few. Every dog's ears are different. Do not expect the cotton to ever come out looking pristine. A little wax actually protects the ear from infection.

Clean your German Shorthaired Pointer's ears about once a week, more often if he suffers from repeated infections or excessive buildup of dirt or wax. Most importantly, always seek veterinary care if you suspect a problem. An untreated outer-ear infection can lead to a more serious inner-ear infection. An infection of this type can be harder to treat and may even cause hearing loss in some animals.

Caring for your GSP's eyes is probably the easiest of all grooming tasks.

Eye Care

Caring for your German Shorthaired Pointer's eyes is probably the easiest of all grooming tasks.

How to Care for the Eyes

Check your dog's eyes daily, and clean them with saline solution about once every week or two or as needed, whichever is more frequent. Simply squirt a small amount of the solution into each eye and wipe any excess that runs down your dog's face with a soft cloth. The saline will flush any dirt and other particles from the eye.

Healthy eyes look bright and shiny. The whites of your GSP's eyes should indeed be white, and the lining of the eyelids should be pink. Signs of a problem include extreme or prolonged redness, inflammation, and colored discharge. Consult your veterinarian if you notice any of these symptoms. A small amount of tearing is normal, but thick, mucus-like secretions are not. Even normal tearstains should be wiped away promptly because they can become a breeding ground for bacteria.

Regular eye cleanings are particularly important if your dog has ectropion (loose lower eyelids), an undesirable but fairly common trait that leaves a dog especially vulnerable to dirt, dust, and other tiny particles like grass and weed seeds. If you hunt with a dog who suffers from ectropion, keep saline on you at all times and remember to flush your dog's eyes periodically.

Dental Care

Your German Shorthaired Pointer needs regular dental care. Neglecting this important task will almost certainly cause your dog to develop periodontal disease, a condition that infiltrates the gum tissue and bone surrounding your dog's teeth. Periodontal disease can also trigger a number of other health problems. Endocarditis, for example, is an infection of the heart valves caused by bacteria from the teeth. Remember, whenever your dog swallows, his saliva carries any bacteria from his mouth throughout his entire body.

If you procrastinate when it comes to caring for your dog's teeth, he will end up needing a professional cleaning by his veterinarian. This process, which requires your dog to be placed under general anesthesia, consists of the teeth being scraped clean with a metal tooth scaler. Preventive care is much easier for both you and your dog, requires no anesthetics or recovery time, and is considerably kinder to your wallet.

How to Care for the Teeth

Ideally, you should brush your dog's teeth every day, but even weekly brushings can make a huge difference in your GSP's oral health. Food residue that is allowed to accumulate on your dog's teeth can morph into plaque and tartar surprisingly quickly. Feeding hard, crunchy food like kibble, biscuits, and raw carrots can clean teeth some, but even these foods leave behind remnants on your dog's teeth.

Some dogs resist having a toothbrush inserted into their mouths. If your dog fits this description, you may use a clean piece of damp gauze on your finger to clean his teeth instead. Just place a pea-sized amount of canine toothpaste on either the brush or gauze and brush one tooth a time, paying particular attention to the area where the tooth meets the gum line. If you are using a conventional brush, hold it at a 45-degree angle for optimum results.

Fortunately, most dogs like the taste of their toothpaste, which comes in a variety of yummy flavors, including beef, liver, and chicken. Unlike human toothpaste, your dog's toothpaste can be swallowed safely, so no rinsing is required. Still, your dog might appreciate a cool drink of water in between your brushing his top and bottom teeth and once again after you have completely finished the brushing

Ideally, you should brush your dog's teeth every day with a canine toothbrush and toothpaste.

task. As with all grooming, praise your dog for his compliance. Positive reinforcement will lead to repeated good behavior.

Chew toys and bones can be great allies for keeping your dog's teeth clean and healthy. Nylabone offers a wide variety of both edible and nonedible bones and chews that satisfy a dog's natural urge to chew while helping to clean his teeth at the same time.

Nail Care

Your dog's toenails will need to be trimmed every few weeks to keep them from growing too long. Overly long

Check It Out

GROOMING CHECKLIST

- ✓ Brush your German Shorthaired Pointer's coat at least once every week to remove dirt, dead hair, and other debris.
- ✓ Bathe your GSP at least once every month or two, more often if he gets into something especially dirty.
- ✓ Trim your dog's toenails a couple times a month, ending with a brisk walk on concrete or pavement to smooth any rough edges.

- ✓ Clean your German Shorthaired Pointer's ears once a week, and keep them as dry as possible to help prevent infections.
- ✓ Inspect your GSP's eyes daily, wiping away any discharge with a damp cloth.
- ✓ Brush your dog's teeth as often as possible. Daily brushings are ideal, but even weekly brushings will help lessen the accumulation of plaque and tartar.

nails can cause a number of painful problems—including breaking, catching on carpeting or clothing, and even being pulled from your dog's foot. Exactly how often your dog will need his nails trimmed will depend on how quickly his nails grow; this can be different for every dog. In general, if you can hear your dog's nails when he walks across the floor, he is already overdue for a trim.

Nail trimming is undoubtedly the most intimidating grooming task for most dog owners. Even if you have absolutely no experience bathing a German Shorthaired Pointer, your chances of making your dog bleed during shampoo time are pretty slim. Some dogs even

enjoy being brushed or blown dry after a bath, but the majority of dogs do not delight in having their nails clipped. The good news is that nail trims do not have to be as bad as many dogs and their owners fear.

How to Care for the Nails

The most important steps for safe nail clipping are to start early and trim often. As soon as you bring your puppy home, expose him to his nail clippers. Let him look them over and sniff them if he wants, but more importantly, use them. In the beginning he may only tolerate having just the nails on a single foot trimmed in one session. If this is the case, try to end on a positive note, and give him a break. Be sure that your dog lets you trim at least a few toenails, though. If you allow him to escape without complying at all, he will think that squirming and fussing will get him out of future trims.

To make your dog more comfortable with having his nails clipped, handle his feet as often as you can. Oftentimes the reason a dog resists nail trims has nothing at all to do with the clipping process itself but rather with having his feet touched. When you increase the

The most important steps for safe nail clipping are to start early and trim often.

amount of time you spend handling your dog's feet, you decrease his discomfort with it—and subsequently his fear of having his nails clipped.

Hidden within your dog's toenail is a highly sensitive area called the nail bed, or quick. If you clip too much of the nail off during a trim, the quick will bleed. This will be painful for your pet and can lead to an infection. Because the quick is so difficult to see on most dogs, it is best to err on the side of caution when trimming your dog's nails. Remove only a small amount of the nail with each trim. Interestingly, the nail bed will actually begin to recede when you trim your pet's nails frequently. This means that you effectively reduce your chances of nipping the quick by making regular nail trims a priority.

To clip your German Shorthaired Pointer's toenails, hold the foot and gently press on the paw pad. This will help extend the nails and make it easier for you to see them. You may then snip off just the hook-like end of each nail.

The two most popular types of nail clippers for a dog of this size are pliers-style clippers and guillotine-style clippers. Both work well, so whichever you choose will be a matter of personal preference. Follow the directions that come with the clippers you choose.

It is a smart idea to take your dog for a walk on asphalt immediately following a nail trim to help smooth any rough edges.

Chapter 6

Training Your German Shorthaired Pointer

Whether you plan to hunt with your German Shorthaired Pointer or keep him exclusively as a pet, you will need to train him. Training not only is necessary but also can be a wonderful bonding activity for you and your pet. At its most basic level, training is about communicating with your GSP, letting him know when he does something you like so that he will repeat that behavior again.

Why Train Your GSP?

The need for some types of training, like housetraining, is more obvious than others. Even new dog owners usually start by teaching their pets where they must go to empty their bladders and bowels. If they do not, their dogs quickly become very unpleasant housemates.

A Pleasant Companion

The need for other types of training can be just as important. Crate training, for example, can be a wonderful aid in housetraining. It can also help prevent your pet from getting hurt or damaging your belongings when you cannot watch him. Socializing your GSP and teaching him basic commands will make him a valued community member. A well-behaved dog is welcome in many more places than an overexcited or aggressive one.

A Safer Companion

In addition to being a more pleasant companion, a well-trained dog is also a safer one. Teaching your German Shorthaired Pointer to come to you when called can literally save his life if he is ever runs away from you in public. Complying with this one command can prevent your dog from running into oncoming traffic, getting too close to a dangerous animal, or becoming lost. You must teach your dog to come to you before you and your GSP find yourselves

Training your dog will make him a safer and more pleasant companion.

in a precarious situation like one of those, though.

An Easier-to-Deal-With Companion

Training your dog can even make tasks like grooming your pet easier for both of you. I learned this firsthand when I was bathing one of my own dogs recently. My dog Damon is not a huge fan of bath day. He tolerates being bathed, but I doubt he will ever truly enjoy it. He doesn't even like walking in the rain. When I call him to the tub, he comes, but grudgingly—walking slowly with his head hanging low and stopping about a foot or two shy of the bathroom door every time. The last time I bathed him, however, I decided to put his training to the test. I realized that once Damon was soaking wet that I had left the ear cleanser and cotton balls in another room. Instead of forgoing his ear cleaning, I decided to tell him to stay in the tub while I retrieved the forgotten items. I knew that I was taking a huge chance, but I felt confident enough in my dog's training to give it a try. When I returned to the bathroom, the reward was mine: Damon was still sitting. Of course, next time I must remember not to lavish praise on him

The most important reason to use positive training is that it is humane—and it also works.

quite so enthusiastically, as all the water that didn't spill onto the floor covered me instead when I hugged him, but nonetheless I had never been so grateful that I had taken the time to teach Damon this simple yet effective command.

Positive Training

Numerous styles of dog training can be used with a German Shorthaired Pointer. Clicker training, for example, is a very popular training method due to its simplicity and effectiveness. Based

THE MOST IMPORTANT TRAINING STEP

W*hat is the most important step in dog training?*
Choose a breed that fits your own personality and lifestyle! Training will be much easier if you start with the right match. If you are an active person with a lot of space, the energetic German Shorthaired Pointer may be ideal for you. Never buy a GSP puppy simply because you think he's cute, though. When a German Shorthaired Pointer won Westminster in 2005, the breed's popularity skyrocketed, causing many fanciers to feel frustrated. Robert Lowe of the Mason-Dixon German Shorthaired Pointer Club in Maryland also operates a rescue group for the breed. As he told the *Washington Times*, "We're delighted one of ours won Westminster. But sometimes breeders cringe when the public only sees the dog under ideal circumstances—on TV or posing on the cover of the L.L. Bean catalog. German Shorthairs are wonderful dogs but not for everyone. That cute puppy can become a 60-pound (27-kg) dog that needs responsible ownership."

on the premise of operant conditioning, clicker training involves the use of a small noisemaking device to reinforce desired behavior. When the dog performs the desired task, the owner offers a small edible reward along with a click. The dog then begins to associate the clicking sound with pleasure. When his experience is pleasurable, a dog is much more likely to repeat a behavior.

The most important reason to use positive training is that it is humane, but another reason is a close runner-up: positive training works. It you make training fun, your dog will be more likely to learn whatever you want to teach him. Keep training sessions short—no more than 15 or 20 minutes. Just five or ten minutes is enough for a puppy. By doing this, you will keep your GSP's interest level high. Also, always try to end each training session on a positive note. If you notice that your dog is becoming tired or bored, set him up for success by making his last task an easy one and laying on the praise so that he looks forward to working with you again once he is refreshed.

Pay attention to your own moods as well. If you are having a bad day, your German Shorthaired Pointer will likely pick up on it, and this could affect his potential for learning at this time. Most importantly, never take out your frustrations from your day on your dog. Take some time to relax before beginning your training session, so you too come to it with a clear head and positive attitude.

Use Praise and Rewards

Whatever form of training you choose to use with your GSP, it should always be positive. Congratulate your dog when he does well by telling him he's a good boy. Your heartfelt praise cannot be underestimated when it comes to training. Even more importantly, though, never admonish your dog for falling short of your expectations. This is the surest way to diminish his interest in whatever you are trying to teach him. Yelling and hitting are fear-inducing behaviors that have no place in any training program. Doing those things will reduce your pet's ability to learn—and likely damage your relationship with him. Your dog should never fear you.

Positive training also involves giving praise for every step in the right direction. Your German Shorthaired Pointer won't become reliably trained in a day or even in a week. If you choose to crate train your dog, for instance, you will have to gradually expose him to the crate before he accepts it completely. Praising him whenever he goes inside it is a great way to reinforce the behavior. By placing a treat inside the enclosure, you increase the chances of having your pet form a positive feeling about the crate, even if he

only stays there long enough to consume the reward.

Use Play

In addition to praise and edible rewards, use play as a means of reinforcing desired behaviors. When your dog reaches a milestone or complies with a particularly difficult command, take a break from training mode to show him exactly how proud you are of him. Hug him, kiss him, tell him what a good boy he is, and jump for joy with him. Some trainers call this "having a party." If your GSP loves squeaky toys, keep one handy as a special reward for a time like this. If he enjoys playing fetch, keep a ball or a flying disc nearby instead. And don't forget to use it. This nonstructured play time, however short, can be the greatest reward you can give your dog.

Socialization

Socializing is one of the easiest of all training tasks, as long as it is done early and consistently.

How to Socialize

All you have to do to socialize your German Shorthaired Pointer is to expose him to as many friendly people and pets as possible. As soon as your dog has had all of his necessary shots, take him with you whenever you go somewhere he can go too. Walk him around your neighborhood during times of the day when others are out and about so that he can meet the masses. Be sure to take a moment to say hello to various people you encounter, preferably asking them to offer your pet a treat to reinforce his good behavior. A full treat bag and a leash are in fact the only necessary tools of the socialization trade. Fill the bag with high-value treats like diced pieces of chicken or hot dogs, something he only gets as a special treat. Soon he will equate strangers with yummy rewards.

Other places you may consider taking your dog include parks, playgrounds, beaches, outdoor landmarks, and your child's sporting events. Kids actually present many ideal opportunities for socializing your new pet. When my son Alec was younger, we lived about a mile (1.5 km) from his school, so I would walk him there and back quite frequently in nice weather instead of driving. Damon, just a puppy at this time, loved accompanying us and greeting everyone we encountered on the way. Even Alec's principal came out to see him one day. As an added bonus, Damon was able to witness all of the other children getting on and off their buses, so he never developed any irrational fears of the loud sounds that large vehicles like those can make.

It's crucial that you socialize your dog to people and other dogs.

A great way to provide your GSP with plenty of dog-friendly company is by inviting friends over to meet your new pet. Throw a homecoming party for your new pet, or invite a few friends at a time to visit over the course of your puppy's first few weeks at home. Be sure to ask everyone to drop by again to keep the socialization going. In addition to being fun for you, entertaining guests regularly gives your dog the opportunity to learn how to behave when a new person enters your home. Encourage your dog to sit quietly beside you at the door as you greet your visitors. You should arm these friends and family members with high-value treats similar to the ones you ask people to offer him in public.

Invite dog-owning friends to bring their pets over to spend time with you and your German Shorthaired Pointer, or make plans to go somewhere together. GSPs get along well with most other dog breeds, but your dog may do best with a dog his own size. In addition to preventing injuries, matching your dog with a similarly sized friend will make it easier for the two of them to keep pace with each other when playing and exploring the great outdoors.

Socialize to People

Socialize your dog to all types of people. Introduce him to adults and children, men and women, tall people and short people, people who wear glasses and hats, people in wheelchairs and on crutches, loud people and quiet people. Be respectful of anyone who doesn't want to meet your GSP. Some people are simply not dog people. While I personally do not understand how anyone could not love a dog, it is important to remember that your dog cannot gain anything from interactions with a person who is uncomfortable around him. If you encounter such a person—be it a friend or stranger—politely move on to someone who does enjoy interacting with the canine species.

When exposing your German Shorthaired Pointer to children, you must be watchful of both the kids and your dog. Not all young people know how to act around dogs, so you may have to explain the rules of gentle play to some children. Sadly, a handful of kids know how to act, but they don't care. Babies and toddlers are too young to understand these rules, so extreme caution must be used when your GSP encounters these tiny humans. No child should ever be left unsupervised with any dog. Even the best-natured dog may bite if a child pulls his ears or his tail or treats him in another inappropriate fashion.

Socialize to Other Animals

You also must use caution when introducing your dog to other animals.

Always ask the owner before you approach another dog at the park or at the beach, for example. Some dogs adore people but dislike other dogs. Some dogs become agitated if another dog approaches them too quickly. Introduce your dog to only one animal at a time, and allow only limited contact until it is obvious that both dogs are at ease with the situation. Most of your German Shorthaired Pointer's interactions with fellow canines will be pleasant, but you must always be on the lookout for the warning signs of a scuffle so that it can be prevented. Growling and the baring of teeth are the most obvious of these red flags, but also listen to your instincts. If you get a bad feeling, it is probably your intuition speaking.

Crate Training

Deciding to crate train your German Shorthaired Pointer can be one of the best decisions you ever make for your pet and the rest of your family. Crate training can be enormously helpful when it comes to housetraining. Because most dogs prefer not to soil the area in which they sleep, keeping your GSP in a crate when you cannot watch him during the housetraining phase can help prevent him from having accidents.

By providing your dog with a crate (or kennel) of his own and training him to use it, you also give him a quiet place to sleep, enjoy a tasty treat, or just spend some time alone when he feels the need. Many dogs clearly see the crate as a special spot of refuge.

Some dogs, on the other hand, have been forced to view the crate quite differently. Dogs bred by puppy mills, for example, may have been forced to spend the early weeks of their lives trapped in kennels, in some cases piled several high. Because these dogs have already been forced to sleep amongst

Some dogs, such as puppy mill or adopted dogs, may have been forced to view the crate as a punishment and harbor fear about it, in which case it is advisable not to use one.

Puppy Love

TAKE A WALK ON THE INSIDE

If you have a hard time teaching your German Shorthaired Pointer puppy to walk with you on a leash, try tethering his lead to your belt while you do chores around the house. Whether you are emptying the dishwasher or folding the laundry and putting it away, this very practical exercise will accustom your dog to getting used to walking with you wherever you go. Use care on stairs so that neither of you trips and falls, and be sure to use a leash that is long enough but not too long—6 feet (2 m) is usually just right.

their own excrement, the potential housetraining benefits of the crate have already been lost. A puppy mill dog may even harbor a downright phobia of the crate. In this situation, I advise owners to forgo using a kennel. Instead, invest in a portable safety gate that you can use to keep your dog in puppy-proofed areas of your home during the training process.

How to Crate Train

If you will be crate training your German Shorthaired Pointer, begin by introducing him to the crate slowly. Situate his kennel in an area of your home where he is likely to encounter it on his own, and place a tempting item such as a toy or treat inside it. Praise him whenever he ventures inside, perhaps even offering him another treat as a reward. Doing this will help your GSP form a positive association with the crate. Be sure to leave the door open so that your dog can walk in and check out

his new digs, and don't close it even after he goes inside. For now you just want him to get acquainted with the crate.

Once your dog is comfortable entering the crate, you may then begin closing the door for short periods—in the beginning just a minute or two. This is usually the point at which some dogs protest, so don't be surprised if your German Shorthaired Pointer fusses when you close the door. The most important thing to remember is that you mustn't let him out to stop him from crying. Wait until he stops, even if it is just for a moment, before opening the door. Gradually increase the length of time you leave him inside the crate with the door closed, continuing to praise and reward him when he behaves well.

Your next step will be leaving the room—again just for a minute or two in the very beginning. If he fusses, wait until he stops before returning to the room. Even if your dog seems to tolerate your absence well, be sure to return promptly. Increase the duration of time that you spend out of sight a little at a time until you think that your dog is ready to spend more than a few minutes in the room all alone. Eventually you should be able to leave him crated long enough to run a quick errand.

No dog should be crated for longer than a few hours, but young dogs who are still in the midst of housetraining must be provided with regular trips to their potty spots between spending time in their crates. You should also give your GSP a chance to stretch his legs and get some exercise between consecutive stints in the crate. I like to take my dogs for a brisk walk before crating them. This usually tires them out, so they can use their time in their kennels to rest up before my return. Likewise, whenever I come home, I try to make time for at least a quick play session after releasing my dogs from their crates and giving them a chance to relieve themselves outside.

Although my dogs have been crate trained for years now, I still make a point of offering them treats inside their kennels occasionally. Just hearing the rattle of our canine cookie jar is often enough to make them run to their crates and sit. Even when I don't offer them their yummy edibles inside the crates, my dogs often take treats there to enjoy them anyway.

Housetraining

Whether you choose to utilize crate training as a part of your housetraining routine or not, the most important step in housetraining your German Shorthaired Pointer will be maintaining a consistent schedule. The ultimate goal of housetraining is to help your pet understand where he should eliminate. In the beginning stages, however, housetraining is really more about training yourself to take your dog to this desired location before he can eliminate elsewhere.

A young puppy's bladder is extremely small, making it nearly impossible for him to wait longer than a couple of hours between trips to his potty spot. A general rule is that a dog should be able to go one hour between elimination trips for each month of age. Therefore an eight-week-old puppy should be taken outside at least every two hours. Although this can seem exhausting to a new pet owner, the good news is that the number of trips you make outside with your dog each day will decrease remarkably quickly. You will be amazed by just how fast that eight-week-old pup grows into a two-year-old dog. This does not mean, however, that an adult German Shorthaired Pointer can go hours and hours without a chance to empty his bladder or bowels. Even the best-trained adult dogs should

The most important step in housetraining your GSP is maintaining a consistent schedule.

be taken outside at least once every six to eight hours.

How to Housetrain

Keep track of when your dog is eating his meals. Most dogs need to eliminate somewhere between 20 and 30 minutes after eating. I recommend using a chart of some sort to record your dog's mealtimes, successful trips to his potty spot, and his accidents. Doing so will help you identify the times when he is most likely to make a mistake. Charts are also a wonderful means of gauging success. In addition to taking your dog outside following his meals, you should

also provide him with an opportunity to eliminate whenever he wakes from a nap and when he has finished a play session. I also recommend removing your dog's water bowl following his meals—just until he is housetrained. Once he "gets it," you can then begin making fresh water available at all times.

When your dog eliminates in the proper spot, praise him. When he makes a mistake, though, refrain from admonishing him. Admonishment will do nothing to teach him what you want from him. The best way to get your German Shorthaired Pointer to repeat a desired behavior is to catch him in the act and let him know that he did well.

If you catch your dog eliminating in the wrong spot—as inevitably you will—interrupt him immediately. Take him to his proper potty spot to finish the job, praising him when he finishes eliminating there. If he seems to be having a hard time making the connection, consider using his potty spot as a place to deposit the fecal matter from his accident, at least temporarily. You may also take a urine-soaked paper towel to this area to

help your dog understand what you want from him. Be sure to remove the excrement after each trip, though, to keep bacteria from accumulating.

If you want to teach your dog to eliminate on command, begin by choosing short phrases, such as "Go pee" and "Go poop," for your dog to relate to those actions. This can be helpful when you want to help your GSP differentiate between a leisurely walk and a trip with a more specific intention—or when you need to be somewhere at a certain time. As soon as your dog begins eliminating, say the phrase that you have chosen to use for that act, praising him when he complies.

Basic Commands

Teach your German Shorthaired Pointer the following commands, one at a time. Once he has mastered the first one, move on to the second. Keep your training sessions short—just a few minutes at a time for a GSP puppy. Short, frequent sessions are preferable to longer, less frequent ones. Your dog will retain more of what he has learned this way, and he will also be more likely to come back to your next training session with a willing spirit.

Watch Me

The *watch me* command is one of the most overlooked tools in dog

The *sit* command is one of the easiest commands for most dogs to learn.

FINDING A TRAINER

Ask your German Shorthaired Pointer's breeder or veterinarian to recommend a reputable dog trainer in your area. You may also contact the Association of Pet Dog Trainers at (800) PET-DOGS or www.apdt.com for the name of a trainer near you. Avoid using the phone book or bulletin board advertisements. Dog trainers do not have to be licensed to perform the work they do, so owners must use extreme care in the selection process. If you do go with someone without a personal or professional recommendation, ask for references, and be sure to follow up by checking them.

The best dog trainers teach owners how to successfully train their pets themselves. In this way, a trainer is really more of a teacher. Because you will be learning right along with your GSP, it is vital that both you and your dog are comfortable with the person you choose. A trainer should always be willing to answer any questions you may have and explain things without talking down to you.

It is important to note that different trainers utilize different forms of training. Popular methods include leash and collar, reward based, and clicker training techniques. Any of these methods can help your German Shorthaired Pointer grow into a happy and well-behaved canine companion. Whatever form of training you choose, make sure that the trainer never uses physical punishment of any kind. Training should always be a positive activity for your dog.

training. Before you teach your German Shorthaired Pointer any other command, consider teaching him this one. If you do, you will always be able to get your dog's attention when you need it—the first step in teaching your GSP anything.

How to Teach It

Holding a treat up beside your face, wait for your dog to look up at you. As soon as he does, say "Watch me," and then give him the treat. Repeat this simple command over and over until you can say just the words to get your dog to look at you. Once your dog has learned this command, use it at the beginning of every training session or when he becomes distracted while working on a specific training task. The *watch me* command can be especially useful when attending a training class with other dogs and their owners vying for your pet's attention.

Sit

The *sit* command is the basis for numerous other basic training commands, which is why I recommend teaching it early. It is also one of the easiest commands for most dogs to learn. Your German Shorthaired Pointer may even know how to do it before you bring him home.

How to Teach It

Grab your treat bag and hold an enticing morsel over your dog's head. Most dogs will naturally go into the *sit* position at this point. If yours does not, resist the urge to push down on his back to make him comply; this could hurt his back. Instead, gently press on the back of his knees to encourage him to bend them into position. As soon as your dog's bottom hits the floor, say "Sit," and give him the treat.

If you are using a clicker, press it at the same time you offer your GSP the treat. Clicking just a moment too soon will reinforce the wrong behavior. If you prefer not to use a clicker, you may say "Good boy!" or "Good sit!" instead. I prefer the latter expression because it directly correlates to the behavior, furthering the dog's understanding of what he did right.

I like to use a hand signal for each command I teach my dogs. The actual signal you use is less important than being consistent about it. I hold my right hand up in a flat position when I instruct my dogs to sit. A good way to test your own hand signal is by omitting the verbal cue once in a while and relying on the

Basic training will result in a better-behaved dog.

visual gesture alone. If your dog sits when you use just your hand signal, you will know that he has learned it. Likewise, occasionally leave out the hand signal to make sure that your GSP knows the verbal command equally well.

Stay

Once you have taught your German Shorthaired Pointer to sit, the next step is to teach him to stay. If I tell my dogs to sit, I don't mind if they stand once I have treated them— unless I have told them to stay.

How to Teach It

Begin by instructing your dog to stay while he is sitting still and praise him for continuing to do so. This is the easiest way to teach your dog the *stay* command. Once your dog seems to understand what staying means, back up slowly after issuing the command. You may also practice the *stay* command by moving around your dog in a circle while he is in the *sit-stay*. Gradually increase the distance you move away from your dog along with the time you keep him in the stay. In the beginning, your German Shorthaired Pointer puppy may stay for only 30 seconds or less, but after some practice, that same dog may be capable of staying for several minutes or more.

When I command my dogs to stay, I use a similar hand signal as when instructing them to sit. Instead of merely putting my right hand up, though, I extend it forward, as a crossing guard might do to tell a driver to stop. To release your dog from the *stay* (or any other) command, choose a word, such as "release" or "free" to let your GSP know when he may move again. Many owners use the word "okay" to release their dogs from commands, but this can prove problematic because many people use this word frequently in normal conversation.

Come

Teaching the *come* command is also easy. Like many other commands, you may begin teaching this one by saying the word whenever you find your dog in the act of moving toward you, praising him when he gets there, of course. Most importantly, never admonish your dog for coming to you—for instance, when he has done something wrong. This is a surefire way to discourage your GSP from complying with the command the next time you use it.

How to Teach It

You can practice this command (also known as the *recall*) by placing your dog on an extra long lead and walking away from him, saying "Come!" in an enthusiastic tone. If you prefer not to use a lead, you may enlist the help of a friend

Check It Out

TRAINING CHECKLIST

✓ Only use positive training techniques. If you make training fun, your German Shorthaired Pointer will always be up for whatever you want to teach him.

✓ Make socialization a part of your dog's earliest training to maintain his friendly temperament.

✓ Utilize a crate to help housetrain your GSP puppy and to keep him out of trouble when you cannot supervise him properly.

✓ Teach your dog basic obedience commands as a foundation for all future learning.

instead, but even if you are indoors or in a fenced yard, you must always have a way of making your GSP comply with the *come* command. Otherwise you will be teaching your pet the wrong behavior.

If you wish to use a visual cue for the *come* command, place both your arms straight out in front of your chest and then wave your hands as you bring them toward your body while saying "Come!" Another great way to encourage your dog to come to you is by bending your knees and lowering your body when instructing him to come to you, somewhat like the posture of the canine play bow. Because many German Shorthaired Pointers are highly food motivated, holding the treat you plan to use as a reward can also be an effective means of enticing your dog to come to you.

Down

All dogs should know the *down* command, but it is especially important for a breed the size of the German Shorthaired Pointer. This command allows you to place your GSP in a calm position when overexcitement could cause a problem. Many owners like to put their dogs in a *down-stay* when welcoming company into their homes to prevent their pets from jumping on their guests.

How to Teach It

To teach your German Shorthaired Pointer to lie down, hold a high-value treat in your left hand while instructing him to sit with your right hand. You may use the voice command as well. Once your dog sits, lower your hand with the treat while bending your right arm from the elbow down. When he lowers his own body into a lying position, say "Down" and offer him the treat.

You may need to kneel down to get your GSP to lie down in the early stages of teaching this command. If this doesn't work, try drawing the treat away from him to encourage him to lower his body. Once he complies with the *down* command, you should then teach your dog to stay in this position—a combination command referred to as a *down-stay*. You can practice the *down-stay* the same way as a *sit-stay*; the only difference is your dog's starting position. Like the *sit-stay*, your German Shorthaired Pointer may only be able to hold a *down-stay* for a short time at first, but with practice he should be able to comply with this dual command for much longer.

Heel

The *heel* command essentially means teaching your German Shorthaired Pointer to walk nicely on a leash on your left side. Start working on this command as soon as you bring your GSP home. If you don't practice good leash etiquette with your cute little puppy now, it will be much more difficult as he grows into a brawny 70-pound (31.5-kg) dog.

Heel is also a combination command. The rules are simple: When you walk, your dog walks, and when you stop, he stops. He should not pull while walking, and he should be ready to resume walking when you are.

How to Teach It

While walking with your dog, stop and say "Sit." After a few seconds, say "Heel," as you begin walking again. The visual clue for heeling is a little more complicated than that of other commands. For starters, it doesn't involve using your hand but instead your foot, specifically your right foot. When you want your dog to walk with you, start off on your right foot. Likewise, if you put him in a *stay*, take off on your left foot when walking away from him. As subtle as it may seem, your dog will pick up on this difference and use it to help him figure out what you want him to do. If you plan to participate in any formal obedience or rally events with your pet, these habits will also come in handy down the road.

Continue to reward your GSP as he learns the various steps involved in heeling. As with all of these commands, you should treat your dog only intermittently for his compliance once he is complying with the *heel* command at least 85 percent of the time, but always praise your pet when he performs the desired behaviors. Continued praise will help ensure ongoing obedience.

Chapter
7

Solving Problems
With Your German
Shorthaired Pointer

If left untrained, your German Shorthaired Pointer may develop a number of unpleasant problem behaviors. Even a well-trained dog can pick up a nasty habit such as barking at strangers if his owner isn't swift in correcting the problem before it becomes a bigger one. The most important thing to remember is that there is no such thing as a bad dog. So-called bad dogs are merely products of their environments and the behaviors they have been allowed to adopt.

Barking (Excessive)

All German Shorthaired Pointers bark sometimes. Unlike people, who can use words to express themselves, dogs use barking as a primary form of communication. You may even want your GSP to bark—when he needs to be taken to his potty spot, for instance. Barking can also be a fun part of play. My own dogs will bark to initiate play, both with me and with each other. It's when barking becomes excessive that it turns into a problem behavior.

Dogs who bark too much aren't a problem for just their owners. They are also a nuisance for anyone else who can hear them. Excessive barking is one of the most common reasons that dogs are surrendered to animal shelters and rescue organizations. When owners cannot stop their dogs from barking too much, the problem can lead to strained relationships with neighbors, eviction notices from landlords, and even fines from your municipality. An owner may even be forced to give up the dog in extreme situations.

Some dogs bark when they encounter people in public places. Others bark at home when visitors arrive. Still others bark when they are left alone. If you listen closely, you will notice that a German Shorthaired Pointer's barks are a lot like a human infant's cries in their specificity. The variations in pitch and tone may be subtle at times, but a perceptive owner can tell the difference between a bark that is meant to show excitement and one that is intended to alert you to a problem. Depending on the type of barking your GSP

If left untrained, your GSP may develop a number of unpleasant problem behaviors.

Puppy Love

ACT EARLY FOR LASTING RESULTS

The good thing about a German Shorthaired Pointer puppy's bad behavior is that he hasn't had enough time for any bad habits to become deeply ingrained. You can usually correct any issues with a puppy's behavior impressively quickly if you are willing to utilize positive training techniques and remain consistent in your approach. Consistency is in fact your best defense against your GSP's developing any further problem behaviors. By training your dog early and practicing what you have taught him repeatedly, you will ensure that your puppy grows into a well-mannered adult dog.

does most, you may have to adjust your strategy for dealing with it.

How to Manage It

One of the best ways to manage your German Shorthaired Pointer's barking is by teaching him the *enough* command. You can do this by catching him in the act of barking and rewarding him when he stops. Wait for the exact moment and say "Enough," as you offer him a high-value treat. Once he makes the connection between his silence and the reward, he will begin responding to this command. Using a clicker may speed this process along.

If you have trouble discerning your dog's moment of silence when he is in the midst of more frenzied barking, try instigating barking at another time when your GSP isn't quite as worked up. Knock on a piece of furniture or make another noise to get your dog to start barking and then follow

the same follow-up steps outlined above. If your dog returns to barking after he receives the treat, wait slightly longer before relinquishing the edible reward the next time he stops barking. You want to stop the barking, not merely change it from being constant to intermittent.

What is most important is that you always wait for him to stop barking (even if it is only for a second) before you say the word and offer the treat. Whatever you do, never use a reward as a bargaining tool to get your dog to stop barking. If you give your German Shorthaired Pointer a treat while he is barking, he may stop long enough to gulp it down, but all he will learn is that barking gets him treats.

Also, never yell at your dog when he barks. Dogs perceive yelling as the human form of barking, so your GSP will think that you are simply joining him in the activity. Say the word "enough" calmly to encourage your dog to match your composure.

A great strategy for preventing unwanted barking is instructing your dog to lie down and stay at times when he is most prone to barking—when you notice the mail carrier's arrival, for example. Most dogs refrain from barking when they are lying down.

You can also discourage unwanted barking in other ways. If your dog barks most at passersby, block his access to windows. If he barks or howls when he is alone, leave the radio or television on when you go out. This will give him something to listen to and also help block out noises that may trigger his vocalization. Never leave your German Shorthaired Pointer chained outside or roaming freely in a fenced yard unsupervised. Boredom, another common trigger for excessive barking, sets in quickly with this intelligent breed, but barking could be the least of your worries. GSPs are adept escape artists and should never be left outdoors unattended.

If your dog's barking is worst around people or other dogs, a little extra socialization will help. Sign up for a training class to give your dog the opportunity to meet people and their dogs in a composed setting. The last class I attended with one of my dogs included a German Shepherd Dog named Sophie whose owner signed her up

A great strategy for preventing unwanted barking is instructing your dog to lie down and stay at times when he is most prone to barking.

for just this reason. At first Sophie seemed very aggressive, barking ferociously at any dog who dared to come near her. By the end of the six weeks, though, Sophie had made friends with every dog in the class and only barked when her owner instructed her to speak.

Chewing

Chewing is not only a normal canine activity but also a necessary one. Puppies need to chew to ease the pain of teething. Older dogs also need to chew to keep their teeth and gums healthy. The problem arises when dogs are allowed to chew things that they shouldn't—items like shoes, children's toys, and furniture. As soon as you come home to find your treasured possessions in tattered remains, chewing changes from a natural pastime into a challenging, even dangerous, behavior. Chewing just one poisonous plant or electrical cord could cost your dog his life.

How to Manage It

The first thing to remember if you are dealing with a chewing problem is that your German Shorthaired Pointer cannot chew what he can't reach. As his owner, it is your responsibility to keep temptations out of sight until your dog understands what is and isn't an acceptable chew toy. This means that every item must have a home. Shoes and other clothing belong in closets. Toys belong in toy boxes. Place other small items

One of the best ways to prevent your dog from chewing your things is by providing him with plenty of exercise and recreation.

behind closed doors or high above your dog's head.

Of course, you cannot protect all of your belongings from your dog's mighty molars. Large items like furniture and rugs cannot be put away easily, although it may be a wise idea to store any items of particular value (either financial or sentimental) until your dog can be trusted not to destroy them. Protect everything else by puppy-proofing your home. Place your GSP into his crate or use a safety gate whenever you cannot supervise him. Whenever possible, use your puppy's leash to tether him to your belt as you go about your daily activities at home.

Provide your dog with plenty of safe chew toys. Sometimes it can take a while to find the right type for your dog. Some German Shorthaired Pointers like solid rubber bones; others enjoy hollow toys that can be stuffed with yummy edibles like peanut butter. If the toy doesn't grab your dog, it won't help keep him from chewing your personal effects. Whatever you do, do not offer your dog anything of yours that he has already destroyed. Even though an item like this is no longer of use to you, passing it on to your pet will only confuse him. Even the smartest dog will have a hard time distinguishing between your brand-new running shoes and the ones he decimated last week. He may even deduce that inappropriate chewing is the fast track to inheriting these items.

One of the best ways to prevent your dog from chewing your things is by providing him with plenty of exercise and recreation. Many dogs chew as a way of relieving boredom. You may notice that your once well-behaved German Shorthaired Pointer suddenly begins taking his frustrations out on your antique furniture if you start leaving him alone too often. You may experience a similar problem if you start skipping your dog's evening walk or his morning playtime.

If you find your dog feasting on an inappropriate item, offer him an acceptable replacement immediately. If he drops the forbidden object in exchange for the substitute, praise him lavishly. For dogs who don't want to compromise, you will have to utilize the *drop it* command. (See sidebar "Teaching *Drop It* and *Leave It*.") For especially stubborn customers, use a high-value treat to help ensure compliance. Likewise, make sure that the *leave it* command is part of your GSP's repertoire. Your dog's teeth are capable of damaging many items in just seconds, so beating him to the punch by instructing him to leave the item alone in the first place may save you the cost of replacing it—and a whole lot of aggravation.

Digging

If your garden is starting to look like a battleground because of your German Shorthaired Pointer's digging, I don't have to tell you why this behavior can be problematic. The good news is that digging doesn't have to be a deal breaker. Like barking and chewing, digging is a very normal canine behavior that can be managed instead of being forbidden.

How to Manage It

Allowing a dog to dig in an appropriate place provides him with a truly canine form of recreation and stress relief. So where is this sacred place in which your dog should be able to dig at will? Right in your backyard! Build your dog his own sandbox especially for digging. A large sandbox made for a child may serve the same purpose, but those can be rather

TEACHING *DROP IT* AND *LEAVE IT*

Teaching your GSP the *drop it* and *leave it* commands is useful not only for preventing him from chewing your belongings but also for helping to ensure his own well-being. Many dangers lurk both inside and outside your home, and like young human children, puppies tend to investigate most new things by placing them in their mouths.

Drop It

To teach your GSP the *drop it* command, grab one of his favorite toys. Begin by holding the toy in one hand with a high-value treat in the other before you toss the toy. As long as the toy that you choose is truly a treasured belonging, your dog's natural reaction will be to go after it. Once he has picked it up, hold the treat out to him as a means of enticing him to drop it. As soon as he does, say the words "Drop it" and give him the treat. He will soon learn to drop whatever he picks up when you issue this important command.

Leave It

Sometimes knowing the *drop it* command isn't enough, though. What if your GSP encounters something that could harm him immediately upon contact—such as a dangerous chemical or a wild

animal? A situation like this is why you also must teach your dog the *leave it* command.

Begin by tossing that same treasured toy in your dog's direction, but instead of allowing him to pick it up this time, interrupt him before he touches it by saying the words "Leave it." If the treat isn't enough to get your dog's attention, move between him and the toy to keep him from reaching it. Reward him as soon as his attention moves from the toy to you. Once he will leave the toy on command, try using a piece of food as the coveted item you toss. This variation works best when you use a different type of food for his reward.

pricey. Even an amateur carpenter can build a basic model with some inexpensive wood, a handful of screws, and a sheet of weed-blocking plastic to prevent vegetation growth. Your dog's sandbox should measure at least 4 by 6 feet (1.3 by 2 m) in area. It should be between 18 and 24 inches (45.5 and 61 cm) deep, so some digging of your own will be required as well.

Situate the sandbox in a shady spot where your dog can spend time without the worry of sunburn or high risk of heatstroke. One of the reasons many dogs dig is to create a cool place to lie in on a hot day. You can buy sand at your local toy store. Some owners mix this sand with the soil they removed when digging. Finally, always cover the box when he isn't using it so that

neighborhood cats cannot use it as an impromptu litter box.

To make your German Shorthaired Pointer's sandbox even more appealing, bury a few treasures within it. Use whatever toys your dog likes best. Certainly you can buy him a few new items, but be sure to include at least one or two well-worn favorites that you only partially bury. Doing so will help encourage him to use the box.

If you catch your dog digging up your garden or other off-limit areas, lead him back to his own sandbox, praising him when he begins digging in this dedicated spot. You can make the sandbox even more inviting by keeping the sand damp. A quick misting with the hose is usually enough to accomplish this task. It is very important that you keep a close eye on your GSP so that you can continue redirecting him if necessary. Eventually he will learn that digging is allowed only in this one area.

House Soiling

House soiling can be one of the most exasperating of all problem behaviors. It is important to differentiate between typical housetraining accidents and intentional house soiling, though. All dogs must be housetrained before they can be trusted not to urinate or defecate on the floor or carpeting. Once a dog is trained, however, accidents should be a thing of the past. No one enjoys stepping in or cleaning up housetraining accidents, but

Allowing a dog to dig in an appropriate place provides him with a truly canine form of recreation and stress relief.

Ask the Expert

PROBLEM BEHAVIOR STUMBLING BLOCK

W*hat is the biggest stumbling block to correcting problem behaviors?* "The big problem is miscommunication," Georgia dog trainer Scott Mitchell told the *Brunswick News.* "People don't understand what their dog is doing, and it can create problems." If you want to correct a problem behavior, you first need to understand why your dog is acting the way he is. Only then can you start changing the behavior.

discovering these messes can be much more frustrating when the perpetrator is a previously reliable animal.

How to Manage It

If the issue is truly a matter of incomplete housetraining, you should be able to correct the problem with remedial training. Immediately implement a new housetraining schedule, complete with a watchful eye and ongoing praise for each success. Also, be sure to continue training until your German Shorthaired Pointer is indeed reliable. There is no such thing as partially housetrained. If your dog is still having accidents, he has not learned what you expect of him.

Implement a Schedule

Begin by considering when your German Shorthaired Pointer is eliminating where he shouldn't. It could be that you are the one who isn't adequately trained. If your dog is going potty outside every morning but you are returning from work to a soiled carpet,

he probably needs to be taken outdoors sometime during the day. No dog should be expected to go more than eight hours between elimination trips. If you cannot make it home on your lunch hour, consider asking a neighbor to take your dog out for you once while you're gone or hiring a professional dog walker.

Whether you are training or retraining your GSP, take him outside as often as possible—ideally every hour on the hour. Use a chart to track your dog's progress and to see where added effort is needed the most. Once he has gone at least a week without eliminating where he shouldn't, gradually increase the time between elimination trips, a half hour at a time.

Accompany Your Dog Outside

Always accompany your dog when he goes outside to do his business. Even if your yard is fenced, it is important that you are there when your German Shorthaired Pointer eliminates. First, it is essential for you to know that he has in fact emptied

PROFESSIONAL HELP

Some problems are too serious to deal with on your own. If your German Shorthaired Pointer is acting aggressively, for example, seek the help of a professional trainer or behaviorist immediately. A dog who suffers from severe separation anxiety also usually needs the help of someone with experience solving this kind of problem. Doing so will help prevent you from inadvertently making the problem worse. Your German Shorthaired Pointer's problem behavior need not be extreme, though, for you to seek the assistance of a professional. If you are feeling overwhelmed from dealing with your GSP's excessive barking or house soiling, for example—no matter how minor it may seem, enlisting the help of someone with more experience can only help you solve the problem more quickly.

his bladder or bowels. Second, as soon as he goes, praise him, allowing him enough time to finish eliminating. You do not want to interrupt him. The one time it is acceptable to interrupt your dog while eliminating is when you have caught him in the act of going where he shouldn't. If this happens, immediately say, "Outside!" while you usher him to the proper elimination spot. Do not punish or admonish him, however. Doing so may make him think that there is something inherently wrong about the act of eliminating.

Clean Up Accidents Thoroughly

And speaking of where your dog is eliminating, consider this as well. It is imperative that you clean any previously soiled areas thoroughly. Remember, your German Shorthaired Pointer's nose is considerably more sensitive than your

own. If he can smell even a trace of a prior accident, he will be much more likely to eliminate in that same spot again. If your dog is eliminating in the same unacceptable area over and over, it may very well be because he can still smell residual urine or fecal matter.

Consider a Vet Checkup

If your GSP was indeed housetrained before the soiling began, you may want to take him for a veterinary checkup. Sometimes a health problem can cause a dog to eliminate where he shouldn't. It could be a bladder or bowel problem or even a food allergy at the root of the problem. Once you have eliminated a physical problem, you can then safely assume that you are dealing with an issue of intentional house soiling.

Intentional House Soiling

Intentional house soiling, or marking, is usually done with urine. This behavior is most common in male dogs, but it is also seen in some females. Your German Shorthaired Pointer may choose to mark an area of your carpet, a piece of furniture, your bed linens, or even his own bed. When a dog marks, he is trying to claim the area or show dominance over the other household members. Marking is frequently seen in households where more than one dog is present.

Marking is a highly instinctual behavior, but it can be discouraged a number of ways. One of the easiest and most effective ways is having your dog neutered as soon as possible. Oftentimes the urge to mark is removed along with the extra testosterone that is eliminated through sterilization. The urge to mark can be especially strong for intact males when a female in heat is nearby.

Many of the same preventive measures that you can use for remedial housetraining can also be used to discourage intentional house soiling. Taking your dog to his potty spot frequently will help minimize intentional house soiling if just because a dog with an empty bladder cannot use urine for marking. Likewise, cleaning up previously soiled areas will dissuade a developing marking habit.

If all else fails, you can help prevent intentional house soiling with a belly band. When this cloth band is wrapped around your dog's abdomen, it will discourage him from emptying his bladder. In many dogs, the belly band is enough to prevent marking altogether. A dog with an especially persistent marking habit may urinate whether the band is on or not, but placing a self-adhesive feminine hygiene pad inside the band can prevent the urine from reaching your carpet or other belongings.

Jumping Up

A friendly dog enjoys greeting people both at home and in public, but an overly excited dog can be a problem. Even small dogs should be taught not to jump on people, but larger breeds like the German Shorthaired Pointer can hurt people by jumping on them. If this behavior is allowed to continue, it can also spiral out of control, making injuries an even more likely outcome—even if all the GSP is trying to do is show enthusiasm for the person on whom he is jumping.

How to Manage It

Like most problem behaviors, the best way to deal with jumping is by preventing it. Teach your dog to sit and wait before you open the door for guests. Instruct your friends and family to offer your pet attention only after he has complied with these commands. Even if they tell you that they don't mind your GSP's jumping, insist that they refrain from speaking to your dog

Check It Out

PROBLEM BEHAVIORS CHECKLIST

✓ Train your German Shorthaired Pointer to stop barking on command by teaching him the word "enough."

✓ The best way to teach your dog not to chew your belongings is by providing him with plenty of appropriate chew toys of his own.

✓ To prevent your GSP from digging up your garden, provide him with a spot of his own where he can dig until his heart is content.

✓ If your dog has a house-soiling problem, schedule an appointment with his vet to rule out a physical cause. If there is none, begin remedial housetraining immediately.

✓ Invite one of your German Shorthaired Pointer's favorite people to help you break a jumping habit. Instruct your dog to sit and wait as you and your friend stage a repeated mock arrival.

✓ Never allow your GSP puppy to place his teeth on you, not even playfully. This will help teach him that biting is an unacceptable behavior. If your dog is showing signs of aggression, seek the help of a professional trainer or animal behaviorist.

until he sits quietly. You may allow your dog to stand when greeting your company as long as he doesn't raise his front paws. If he does, command him to sit and wait again. Eventually your dog will sit politely without even being asked each time someone arrives at your door.

If your German Shorthaired Pointer has already developed a jumping habit, you can start correcting this behavior by holding practice greetings with your dog and his favorite people. Stage these encounters in different locations so that your dog understands that he is expected to behave well both at home and places like the dog park, the pet supply store, and while walking on a leash around your neighborhood. In the beginning, keeping your pet on his leash may be necessary both in public and at home, but as he starts to make progress, you can practice without the leash in safe places.

Using visual clues for the *sit* and *wait* commands may be helpful, especially if your dog barks when he hears a doorbell or knocking—or if he just has a hard time listening to you when he gets excited. Another useful trick is the body block.

When your dog starts to lift his paws off the floor, move your body into the space so that he is forced to move backward. In most cases this will interrupt the jumping. Turning away from a jumping dog has a similar effect.

If you do not want your dog to jump on other people, you mustn't allow him to jump on you. Make sure that everyone in your household understands the rules. If just one person tolerates jumping, it can make breaking this unpleasant habit a much more difficult challenge.

Nipping and Biting

Biting is the most serious of all canine problem behaviors. In addition to being dangerous for anyone who comes into contact with your dog, biting can also be dangerous for your German Shorthaired Pointer himself. Aggressive behaviors like biting can trigger nasty fights between your dog and other animals. It can also lead to lawsuits and criminal charges for you. If your dog bites someone, you could even be forced to euthanize your precious pet.

How to Manage It

When it comes to biting, an ounce of prevention is definitely worth that proverbial pound of cure. The best thing you can do for your German Shorthaired Pointer puppy is to socialize him properly to help ensure that he retains a friendly temperament as he moves into adulthood. Many dogs who act aggressively around strangers are actually reacting to their own fear. Usually these dogs haven't spent enough time around new people to realize that there is no reason to be scared of them. Dogs who have been socialized to people early and often, however, are usually completely at ease in the company of others.

In addition to introducing your German Shorthaired Pointer to as many people (and other pets) as possible, use playtime as an opportunity to show your dog what is and isn't acceptable canine behavior. Never allow your dog to place his teeth on your skin, not even playfully. If he tries, pull your hand away at once. You may offer him a chew toy instead and praise him if he takes it from you. And be sure to let everyone else who plays with your dog know that even good-natured biting isn't allowed.

Aggressive biting is a much more serious matter. Fortunately, this type of biting usually comes with warning signs, like growling and baring teeth. If you pay attention, you can reverse the problem before it becomes a much bigger one. You mustn't ignore these important signals. Seek professional help immediately.

Chapter
8

Activities With Your German Shorthaired Pointer

Advanced training activities can help provide your German Shorthaired Pointer with two of the things he needs most: exercise and time with you. Perhaps your GSP came from a long line of conformation champions. If so, showing may be the activity for the two of you. Maybe he was the star pupil of his first obedience class. If that is the case, you both may enjoy competing in rally competitions. Whichever activity you prefer, spending recreational time with your pet will deepen your bond and likely lead to a whole lot of fun in the process.

Traveling With Your GSP

If you like to travel, your German Shorthaired Pointer may be an ideal companion. While it may not be practical for your dog to accompany you on a business trip or a trip to the city, many other travel destinations suit the GSP just fine. A week at the beach or the lake, for example, can be just as relaxing for your pet as it is for you.

Before You Go

Most dogs much prefer the minor inconveniences of traveling to the most common alternative: boarding. As your GSP's owner, however, it is your responsibility to make sure that he is safe and comfortable, both along the way and once you arrive at your destination.

SPORTS AND SAFETY

Always be on the lookout for signs that your German Shorthaired Pointer needs a break. No matter how much your dog enjoys a particular activity, too much of anything can be a bad thing. When your dog appears to be losing steam, offer him some time off. Take him to his potty spot, and give him a fresh drink of water when he's done. It is imperative that your GSP gets regular rest and stays hydrated when competing in organized activities, as well as when he is practicing for them. Mental respites are also important. If your dog appears to be losing interest in practicing flyball moves or obedience commands, offer him some time away from the activity. Give him a toy that can be stuffed with an edible goodie like peanut butter, or rub his belly while you take a break yourself and watch a movie. In addition to being exhausting, overexercising can lead to injuries. Your dog will also be more likely to return to his favorite activity with a positive attitude if he is given regular physical and mental breaks.

German Shorthaired Pointers are athletic dogs who excel at many types of activities.

Get a Vet Checkup
Whether you will be driving or flying, the first step in planning any vacation that includes your pet is a veterinary checkup. If your dog has any health issues, the time to address them is before you embark on your holiday. If he takes medication regularly, you also want to make sure that you have enough to last throughout your trip. Additionally, depending on the location of your destination, your dog may need certain vaccinations or other preventive care prior to traveling. For instance, if you live in a colder climate, your dog may not be on a year-round heartworm preventive. If you are heading south, he will need to

start taking this medication once again prior to embarking on your adventure.

Make a List
Next, make a list of all the things your German Shorthaired Pointer may need while away from home. Keep it as short as possible, but be sure not to overlook anything important. Generally a traveling GSP will need a crate with a liner, a set of bowls, his food and a thermos for water, his leash and collar (complete with identification tags), and proof of all necessary vaccinations. I also recommend keeping a box of plastic zip bags with you at all times because they

can serve multiple purposes—including cleaning up after your pet in pubic places. Don't forget to include some items for entertainment, too, such as toys and bones. Finally, always pack a canine first-aid kit when traveling with your pet.

Travel by Car

Never leave your GSP, or any other animal, alone in a vehicle. Temperatures inside a closed car can skyrocket faster than many dog owners realize, leaving their pets exposed to dangers such as heatstroke. Every year thousands of dogs die as a result of being left inside unattended vehicles. Don't let your beloved GSP become one of them.

Confine Your Dog

If you will be traveling by car, the first thing you must do is decide where your German Shorthaired Pointer will be riding. If you have the space, the safest place for your dog during the trip is in his crate. If you must collapse his crate for transport, be sure to invest in a canine seat belt made for a dog of your GSP's size. Most pet supply stores sell these simple devices, which can save a dog's life in the event of a crash. A seatbelt not only protects your precious

Make sure that your German Shorthaired Pointer is a welcomed guest when making your travel arrangements.

pet but also helps to keep both you and your other travel companions safe. If you are involved in a traffic accident, your dog could be thrown into another passenger, injuring both him and the person he hits. Keeping your dog in his crate or in a seat belt also prevents him from getting into mischief during the ride, something that could cause an accident.

Take Frequent Breaks

Be sure to take frequent breaks when traveling by car with your pet. This will give your German Shorthaired Pointer the opportunity to stretch his legs a bit, enjoy a drink of water, and relieve himself when necessary. He will be a much more pleasant companion if he isn't cooped up in a car for eight hours straight.

Carsickness

If your dog tends to get sick when riding, feed him at least two hours before setting out on your trip. Cracking a window and placing your dog's crate so that he can see outside the vehicle can help prevent the onset of motion sickness. Your vet may also be able to prescribe a preventive medication to help avert this common canine ailment. In minor cases, a small amount of ginger may be helpful. You can find crystallized ginger at your local grocery store, or you can give your dog a couple of gingersnap cookies just prior to leaving.

Travel by Air

If you will be traveling by plane, it is especially important that you plan every detail of your German Shorthaired Pointer's trip.

Find Out the Airline's Rules

When purchasing your tickets, talk to a representative from the airline about its rules regarding canine passengers. Your GSP will likely need to have a rigid-style crate, but he may also need to have very specific documents affixed to his kennel during the trip. Smaller breeds are often allowed to ride in the cabin with their owners, but your German Shorthaired Pointer's size will require him to ride in the baggage compartment. Because it can be difficult to regulate the temperature in this area of the plane, some airlines do not allow animals to ride there at certain times of the year.

Also, check with a person of authority in the area of your destination to make sure that your dog will be welcome in the municipality you will be visiting. International laws relating to pet travel can be complicated and can also change periodically. The worst time to find out that your dog cannot accompany you on your trip is upon arriving at the airport on the day of your flight.

Prepare the Crate

Be sure to affix a bowl of water to the inside of your dog's crate so that he stays hydrated during the flight. The door should be kept closed, but do not lock it. In the event of an emergency, the airline employees must be able to get to your pet quickly. Always attach identification to both your dog's collar and his crate—including your name and cell phone number—so that you can be reached on the spot if there is indeed a crisis.

Pet-Friendly Lodging

Whether you will be spending your vacation time at the home of family or friends, staying in a hotel, or renting a house or condo, you must make sure that your German Shorthaired Pointer is a welcomed guest when making your travel arrangements. Never assume that your dog can go wherever you go. Perhaps your Aunt Helen is allergic to dogs, or maybe your friends with the spacious guest room also have a cat who isn't at all fond of dogs.

Use the Internet

If it is pet-friendly lodging you seek, the Internet can be one of your best resources. Websites like www.takeyourpet.com and www.dogfriendly.com list thousands of hotels and other establishments around the United States that accept canine guests. Look for sites that allow previous guests to leave reviews of their experiences, and read as many as you can before selecting a place for your stay.

If You Can't Take Your Dog

If you must leave your German Shorthaired Pointer behind, ask a family member or friend to stay home with your dog while you are away. If you have trouble finding someone to do this, consider employing a pet sitter or using a boarding kennel instead. Your veterinarian should be able to suggest a reputable business of this kind, or you can ask dog-owning friends for recommendations.

Professional pet sitters either stop by your home at various times each day or stay overnight with your dog while you're gone. Because you will be trusting this caregiver with both your precious pet and keys to your home, you must be comfortable with the person you choose. You may even have to interview several different people before finding the one who is just right for the job. Ask for references, but most importantly, listen to your own instincts. Even if a specific sitter has an impeccable resume, if you have a bad feeling about her, keep looking.

Many veterinarians offer boarding services for their clients, but this option is practical only if you will be away just a short time. If you will be gone for more than a day or two, consider a boarding facility that offers more than basic care and feeding. Choose one that offers daily socialization with other dogs and fun physical activities like games. Many of

Puppy Love

AGILITY ISN'T FOR PUPPIES

If your energetic German Shorthaired Pointer puppy seems destined for agility competition, you will have a few months to attend some events and work with your dog informally before making a final decision. Unlike obedience, you see, a dog must be 12 months old to compete in agility. Although dogs must be physically fit for either activity, agility is considerably more strenuous on a dog's body than obedience. Because a puppy's growing bones and ligaments are weaker than an adult's, the potential for injury is lessened substantially by waiting this reasonable amount of time.

You can, of course, start introducing your dog to agility obstacles at any age. Encouraging a young dog to run through chutes or tunnels, for instance, may very well help him avoid any fear of these objects later. Do avoid any tasks involving jumping, though, until your dog is older. If you would like to at least familiarize your puppy with bar jumps, you may simply lay one bar on the ground and have your dog walk over it instead of jumping over it.

these businesses refer to themselves as canine camps or spas. Some even use webcams so that owners can check in on their pets and see for themselves how they are doing during their stay. Ask for references from these facilities as well. After all, you can only enjoy your trip if you know that your German Shorthaired Pointer is in good hands at home.

Sports and Activities

Sports and other organized activities are a fun way to provide your German Shorthaired Pointer with the exercise and mental stimulation he needs. These pastimes can be a whole lot of fun for you too.

Agility

An excellent opportunity for combining exercise and mental stimulation, agility is also a truly interactive sport in which dogs navigate a timed obstacle course. Although the sport of agility has only been recognized here in the United States since 1994, it was actually developed in England back in the 1970s. Resembling equestrian jumping competitions, canine agility courses consist of similar obstacles, but they are built to a smaller scale.

One thing that certainly isn't downsized, however, is the fun. Agility competitions have quickly become an amazingly popular pastime in this country for both participants and a mass of mesmerized onlookers. As handlers run alongside their dogs, the canine athletes make their way over colorful bars, vaulted walks, and seesaws. Keep watching and you will see the same dogs dash through A-frames, suspended tires, and tunnels. Handlers may assist their pups by offering hand signals, verbal commands, or both.

All dog breeds (and mixes) are welcome to participate in agility. This is ultimately where the similarities of agility and obedience end, though. One distinctive difference that many agility enthusiasts tout as an advantage of their pastime is the amount of handler involvement allowed in this sport. Agility handlers are permitted to talk to their dogs, redirect them verbally, or cheer them on at any time.

Once ready for competition, your dog will be entered in the novice class. Succeeding at this level will earn your dog a Novice Agility Dog (NAD) title. Subsequent titles are then available in the following order: Open Agility Dog (OAD), Agility Dog Excellent (ADX), and Master Agility Excellent (MAX). In order to obtain each title, a dog must earn a qualifying score in the respective class on three separate occasions and from two different judges. Issuance of the MAX title is dependent upon ten qualifying scores in the Agility Excellent Class.

Canine Good Citizen® Program

One of the best platforms for any advanced training activity—and truly an accomplishment within itself—is the completion of the AKC Canine Good Citizen (CGC) program. A certification series begun in 1989, the CGC program stresses responsible pet ownership by rewarding dogs who display good manners both at home and in the community. Those interested may attend the CGC training program, an optional class offered to owners and their dogs, before taking a very detailed ten-step test. Upon completion, certificates are awarded.

The CGC program focuses primarily on a dog's obedience skills and temperament, but it also stresses the importance of serious owner commitment. All owners are required to sign a Responsible Dog Owners Pledge before taking the test. This unique document states that the owner agrees to effectively care for the dog for the rest of the animal's life. It also encompasses such important areas as health and safety, exercise and training, and basic quality of life. It even addresses such community-based issues as agreeing to clean up after your pet in public and never allowing your dog to infringe on the rights of others.

A dog who passes this valuable examination is awarded an AKC certificate complete with the CGC logo embossed in gold. CGC certification can also be useful to your dog in many other areas of advanced training. A dog worthy of the revered title of Canine Good Citizen is

In a conformation show, the dog is judged against his breed standard.

considered a responsible member of his community, a community that includes both people and dogs whom he already knows and all of those he will encounter in the future.

Although dogs of any age may participate in the CGC program, puppies must be at least old enough to have had all necessary immunizations. To ensure that your dog's certification is reliable, it is strongly recommended that younger dogs who pass the test get retested as adults because temperaments and abilities can possibly change during this formative period. All breeds (as well as mixed breeds) are welcome in the program.

Conformation (Dog Showing)

Dog shows, also called conformation events, evaluate just how closely the entrants match their breed's standard, an indication of an animal's ability to produce quality puppies. Showing began in fact as a means of evaluating breeding stock; therefore, spayed and neutered dogs may not participate. A member of the American Kennel Club's Sporting Group, the German Shorthaired Pointer is no stranger to the ring. The breed has been formally shown in the United States for more than 80 years.

Before a GSP or dog of any other breed can be entered in a conformation show, he must meet certain criteria. A complete list of rules and regulations governing eligibility may be obtained from the AKC, but basic guidelines require that your dog be a purebred German Shorthaired Pointer, AKC registered, and at least six months old. Show dogs cannot have registration papers that limit their breeding, but a breeder may change a limited dog's status by making a written request to the AKC.

Shows can range in size and variety from small local specialty events to national all-breed shows with more than 3,000 entrants. Even if you have no plans of ever showing your German Shorthaired Pointer, attending a large-scale AKC conformation event can be an amazing experience for any true dog fancier. At no other place will you ever see so many different breeds all in one place, many of which you may have never seen previously.

Breeds are divided into seven groups: sporting dogs, hounds, working dogs, terriers, toys, non-sporting dogs, and herding dogs. Each dog is then placed in one of five classes: Puppy, Novice, Bred by Exhibitor, American-Bred, and Open. Males are always judged first. Once a German Shorthaired Pointer is judged best of breed, that dog then goes on to represent the breed in the group competition.

Dogs accumulate between one and five points with each win. The number of points awarded depends on the number of dogs in competition, the location of the event, and several other factors. Shows awarding three or more points are considered majors. A total of 15 points is necessary for championship status. When a dog reaches this level, he has earned the title of Champion (abbreviated as Ch.) to be used before his name thereafter.

If you are interested in participating in conformation events, begin by first attending shows as a spectator. If the grooming area is open to the public, introduce yourself to the other German Shorthaired Pointer owners there and ask whether they would mind telling you about their experiences with showing. Although this is a competitive

German Shorthaired Pointers enjoy sharing in activities with their owners.

Ask the Expert

THE NEED TO HUNT

Do German Shorthaired Pointers need to hunt?

German Shorthaired Pointer Club of America (GSPCA) member Charlene Rutar is a GSP breeder from Indiana. As she explained to me, "They need to work but not necessarily hunt. Just about any type of dog–human joint activity will suffice: canine performance events, tracking, search and rescue, frisbee and dance routines, stupid dog tricks for birthday parties—you name it. If you don't give them enough to do, they will make up games and projects of their own. Their prey drive is impressive, though, which is why hunting is a natural for them."

environment, there are many extremely kind and outgoing people involved in the activity who are willing to help newcomers and who also enjoy sharing their enthusiasm for the breed with other kindred spirits.

If you have already purchased your dog, consider joining your local German Shorthaired Pointer club. You will likely find that the organization offers classes for conformation training. Entering this sport and absorbing all the necessary information can be overwhelming. By taking it slowly and learning as much as you can, you will help ensure a positive experience for both you and your dog.

Flyball

Flyball is an exciting canine sport that requires both speed and dexterity. Upon hearing a signal, the dog's owner releases him on the flyball course, a small and straight strip of land. His goal is to run over four hurdles to the end of this course, where a box with a trap and foot lever awaits him. The dog then jumps onto the foot lever, releasing a tennis ball into the air. After he has leapt to catch this ball, he then darts back to his owner with the ball. This is all timed down to the second. Typically flyball is a team sport, consisting of two to four relay teams of four dogs per team. Dogs may compete on either single-breed or multi-breed teams.

Flyball is a particularly fun pastime for dogs ready to take regular ball playing to the next level. A great number of dogs competing in flyball are members of the AKC's Herding Group, but all breeds (and even mixed breeds) are allowed to play on multi-breed teams. Many German Shorthaired Pointers can give even the fastest Border Collie a run for his money at this fast-paced canine sport.

Hunting and Field Trials

If your German Shorthaired Pointer has retained the breed's love of the hunt, field trials may offer him an exciting opportunity to get back to his roots. Styled after traditional game hunts, these exciting events provide a unique chance for owners and dogs to compete together in this oldest canine sport. An individual event may be open to multiple sporting breeds or limited to just one. Championship points are issued only in the latter case, though.

GSPs unquestionably can still hunt the old-fashioned way. The purpose of field trial clubs is to prepare sporting dogs for either activity, so a dog trained through

one of these organizations should be capable of vying for titles and putting food on his owner's table.

If you think that you might enjoy competing in this sport with your German Shorthaired Pointer, get him involved as young as possible. You can have a puppy tested for so-called birdiness before deciding whether this is the dog for you. Many kennels breed with this hunting purpose in mind; you will probably have the best luck finding a GSP well suited to this activity by purchasing a dog from one of these breeders.

Like formal obedience trials, field trials offer several levels of competition with a respective point system for each, but the specifics are a bit more complicated for this activity. The number of other breeds involved in a particular event and even an individual dog's age, for example, can play important roles. A good breeder experienced in this sport should be able to help guide you through the process.

Field trials may offer your German Shorthaired Pointer an exciting opportunity to get back to his roots.

Obedience

For many dog owners, advanced training in obedience begins with a relatively casual level of involvement—taking your German Shorthaired Pointer to a basic obedience class as a puppy, for instance. You may even decide to check out competitive obedience after working with your dog privately to teach him a few commands you think he should know. In many cases, though, both dog and owner discover that this seemingly stoic style of training can actually be a really fun pastime for all involved. Advanced obedience training, when properly implemented, is simply higher education for your GSP.

In obedience competition, the first class you will enter is the novice class, also called the Companion Dog (CD) class. This beginning level focuses on demonstrating the skills of a good canine companion—heeling both on and off the leash at different speeds, coming when called, and staying for fixed periods while also remaining still and quiet with a group of other dogs. Your dog will also be required to stand for a basic physical examination by the judges. Next comes the open class. This second tier of obedience is also called the Companion Dog Excellent (CDX) class. In this level, your dog will need to repeat many of the same exercises from the novice level, but off his leash and for longer periods. Jumping and retrieving tasks are also included in this phase.

The utility level, which provides your GSP with a Utility Dog (UD) title, is for dogs nearing the top of their obedience game. In this stage your dog will need to perform more difficult exercises complete with hand signals, as well as scent discrimination tasks. Once your dog can perform at this level, he can then go on to pursue the highest possible titles of Obedience Trial Champion (OTCh) and Utility Dog Excellent (UDX). Both are very prestigious titles and neither easily nor quickly achieved.

Like the CGC program, obedience is considered by many German Shorthaired Pointer enthusiasts to be a great foundation for many other canine activities. Maybe your ultimate plan is for your dog to become a therapy dog, or perhaps you just want to participate in a fun weekend pastime together, with any awards being just an added bonus. No matter what obedience means to you and your dog, bear in mind that succeeding does not mean that your dog must earn all available titles. As with any other activity, there is nothing wrong with striving toward your next goal, but the most important thing is enjoying the road that leads there. Any owner of a German Shorthaired Pointer who earns a CDX or UD title should be very proud, as these are very reputable accomplishments.

Rally Obedience

Rally obedience differs from conventional obedience trials in that it combines obedience work with the faster pace and performance stations of agility work. Depending on the level of competition, a dog competing in rally may be expected to perform between 12 and 20 different obedience commands (or combination of commands) at each station. Each dog

Check It Out

SPORTS AND ACTIVITIES CHECKLIST

✓ When traveling with your German Shorthaired Pointer, always make your arrangements in advance.

✓ Make an appointment with your dog's veterinarian for a quick checkup to make sure that your GSP is in shape for travel, and stock up on any medications you will need while away.

✓ When traveling by plane, contact the airline, the tourism office of your destination, and the person handling your accommodations to make sure that your German Shorthaired Pointer is a welcomed guest wherever you plan to take him.

✓ If you are considering showing your German Shorthaired Pointer, attend a local conformation event and talk to the GSP breeders and handlers there. Most are more than willing to talk about their favorite subject—German

Shorthaired Pointers—once their dogs are done in the ring.

✓ If you think that your dog has what it takes to become a therapy dog, have him take the Canine Good Citizen test and request an evaluation by Therapy Dogs International (TDI).

✓ Sports like agility and flyball can be a lot of fun, as can formal obedience trials and rally events. Watch your German Shorthaired Pointer for signs of where his interests lie before committing to a particular sport. Your dog may not be suited to one activity, but he could be an ideal competitor in another.

✓ If you are interested in competing in field trials or hunting with your German Shorthaired Pointer, let potential breeders know. They can help you select a GSP who would be the best choice for this activity.

begins with a total of 100 points; he keeps these points by correctly performing the various commands. Each dog is also timed, but this number becomes relevant only if two dogs earn the same score at the end of the event. Rally has become an increasingly popular pastime in recent years. Like the CGC program, it is considered a practical

springboard for therapy work and other advanced activities.

The three levels of rally obedience are Novice, Advanced, and Excellent. Novice is for beginners and is the only level that allows dogs to remain on leash while performing their various commands. Owners also are allowed to clap their hands or pat their legs as they move through the course with their dogs. The Advanced level removes the leash from the equation and adds more stations into the mix. The Excellent level, the most difficult of the three, allows neither leashes nor physical encouragement on behalf of the owners and includes the highest number of stations. The dogs with the four highest scores in all three levels earn ribbons or commemorative rosettes—first place is blue, second is red, third place is yellow, and fourth is white. A dog and handler must earn a minimum score of 70 points to qualify for one of these awards.

Therapy Work

At the end of a bad day, I am always especially grateful to have my dogs by my side. Even if nothing else has gone right, they make me laugh and remind me not to take life too seriously. If I'm feeling ill, they remain steadfastly by my side, getting my mind off whatever is ailing me. They even make good days all that much better. I'm sure many of you can relate to these scenarios, as almost all dogs offer a similar boost for their beloved owners.

An American nurse named Elaine Smith took this means of raising a dog lover's spirits to a whole new level. While working in England, Smith noticed the positive effect that pets had on patients when they visited them alongside human friends and volunteers. These interactions were the inspiration for the organization Smith founded when she returned to the United States in the late 1970s: Therapy Dogs International (TDI).

For decades, studies have shown that Smith's observations went far beyond merely elevating a patient's mood, a worthy effort in itself. For people who love dogs, sometimes just being around this unique species is enough to stimulate physiological changes in their health. Very real changes in mental health also have been observed.

Dogs of any breed, as well as mixed breeds, can be therapy dogs. Perhaps you think that your German Shorthaired Pointer has what it takes to join the ranks of these canine Florence Nightingales. Many GSPs indeed perform this important and rewarding work.

Certification begins with a test by a TDI evaluator. A dog must be at least a year old at this time and possess a sound temperament. Passing the AKC's Canine Good Citizen test is also a prerequisite. A potential therapy dog's behavior is observed around both people and service equipment, such as crutches and wheelchairs. A health record form must be completed by the dog's veterinarian as well. Like a doctor's, a therapy dog's first responsibility is to do no harm to the patients he visits. For more information, visit the Therapy Dog International website at www.tdi-dog.org.

Health of Your German Shorthaired Pointer

I f you feed your German Shorthaired Pointer a healthy diet, provide him with plenty of exercise, and groom him regularly, you have already begun making his good health a priority. Another important step in keeping your GSP in tip-top shape is selecting a knowledgeable veterinarian to help you care for your pet. By taking your dog for regular visits to the vet, you will make sure that any health problems that he experiences can be addressed as efficiently as possible.

Finding a Vet

At one time every area seemed to have its own veterinarian—and usually just the one. If you lived in a particular town, you took your dog to the vet who ran the practice there. Today, however, dog owners have numerous veterinary care options, even within their city limits. Some owners prefer vets who use the latest technological tools. Other people want holistic veterinarians who provide complementary medicine like acupuncture and homeopathy. Some want vets who will make house calls. Depending on where you live, you may even be able to find a single veterinary hospital that offers all of these services and more.

Ask for Recommendations

Unless you will be buying or rescuing a German Shorthaired Pointer from far away, ask your breeder or rescue volunteer to suggest a good veterinarian. I have found that recommendations from these individuals are wonderful tools for finding caring, capable vets. Although you may be tempted to reach for the telephone book or run an online search to find a vet in your area, you will get much better information from someone who knows the GSP breed the best than you will from a Yellow Pages ad or a website.

Fellow German Shorthaired Pointer owners can also be great resources for finding the right vet for your dog. If you know people who own GSPs, ask them how they like their veterinarians. Avoid

Unless you will be buying or rescuing a German Shorthaired Pointer from far away, ask your breeder or rescue volunteer to suggest a good veterinarian.

Ask the Expert

CONVENTIONAL AND HOLISTIC VETS AND DOCTORS

*W*hat is the biggest difference between conventional veterinarians and those who use a holistic approach?

Dr. Monique Maniet founded Veterinary Holistic Care in Besthesda, Maryland, in 1995. As she explained to the *Washington Post*, "Traditional doctors are more trained to suppress symptoms and make them disappear. We look at the underlying cause and stimulate the body to heal itself."

asking yes or no questions, but instead ask things like "What do you like best about your dog's vet?" If they struggle to answer this question, continue your search. People will have plenty of good things to say about an excellent vet or hospital.

Use the Internet

Once you have gathered a few recommendations, this is the time to turn on your computer. Visit each hospital's website (most hospitals have one) to get basic information such as location, hours, and fees for basic services. Some sites even offer virtual tours of the hospital's facilities. State-of-the-art technology may be considered a perk, but don't be fooled by fancy waiting rooms with expensive furniture and high-end decor. The cost of these superfluous extras gets passed along to a business's clients. What is most important is that the hospital is neat, clean, and well organized.

Most websites also include bios for each veterinarian. Where a particular vet went to school or what organizations the vet belongs to may not matter to you, but I highly recommend reading this information anyway. Usually you can also learn about each vet's specialties and areas of specific interest—including which kinds of pets the vet owns. A vet who breeds German Shorthaired Pointers or serves as an AKC judge for the breed, for instance, could be an ideal match for you and your GSP. Certainly your vet doesn't need to be heavily involved with your particular breed, but a vet who has an obvious love of dogs in general is a great candidate for your business.

Stop by the Clinic

Unfortunately, you cannot get a true feel for a veterinarian or a hospital from photographs or write-ups. Nothing takes the place of meeting a vet and seeing a hospital's facilities for yourself. Once you have a potential veterinarian in mind, I recommend stopping by the hospital unannounced to make your first appointment. Doing this will give you the opportunity to meet the support staff. Remember, you will be dealing with these people both on the phone and in person every time your German Shorthaired Pointer visits his vet. Are they friendly and obvious animal people? Are they knowledgeable and helpful, or are they overworked and easily frazzled? You mustn't expect them to drop everything and give you an immediate tour, but choosing a busy time of day for this initial visit will give you the best insight into how the hospital runs.

Dropping in to set up an appointment will also allow you to see whether the online image of the hospital matches up to the actual facility. Are the floors clean? Are there separate waiting areas for sick pets and those being seen for well visits? Is the phone answered promptly when it rings? Do clients seem surprised by the cost of services rendered when paying their bills? Your top priorities may differ somewhat from another owner's, but you will be amazed by how much information you can gather in just this short time period.

Regular exercise and good nutrition will help keep your dog healthy.

If you get a bad feeling, leave without making an appointment. Even if you can't seem to articulate the problem, you may be picking up on something important. Every one of us has a certain amount of intuition about people. I recommend heeding it, especially when it comes to choosing caregivers for our precious pets. It is essential that you be comfortable with the person and hospital you choose.

I also recommend bringing your German Shorthaired Pointer with you when stopping by the hospital this first time. Your dog's reactions to the people and surroundings can be especially telling. Not all dogs enjoy going to see the vet, but your dog shouldn't have an adverse reaction to any of the staff. If he does, this too could be a red flag.

Schedule an Initial Checkup

If you like what you see, go ahead and schedule an initial checkup for your GSP. Make a list of all of the questions the hospital's website doesn't answer, and take this along with you to your appointment. You may want to ask what types of lab work are performed on site. Many hospitals now have the ability to get test results for common afflictions such as heartworm and Lyme disease in mere minutes. When vets send lab work to outside agencies, the turnaround time can be several days instead. I also recommend asking whether there is

a staff member on site to care for pets staying overnight. What is the hospital's protocol for dealing with emergencies? Can the staff provide you with the name of a good emergency clinic for those times when the hospital is closed? You also might have questions more specific to your GSP relating to his diet, housetraining, or anything else.

Your vet should be willing to listen to your concerns and answer any question you have about your dog's care. You mustn't expect your vet to always know everything, but a doctor who doesn't immediately have the answer you seek should be willing to find it for you. Beware of a vet who rushes through your appointment. Remember, you are paying for the time spent with you and your dog. Also, beware of a vet who talks down to you. You and your veterinarian will be the two most important people in your German Shorthaired Pointer's life when it comes to his health. The vet you choose should see you as a partner in this endeavor.

Annual Vet Visit

Whether you bought your German Shorthaired Pointer puppy from a breeder or adopted an adult dog, he will have already begun the vaccination process before you bring him home. You may need to return to the vet for any necessary booster shots during his first few months at

An annual vet visit is crucial to keeping your GSP in good health.

home, though. Once your GSP has seen his vet for an initial checkup and is up to date on all his inoculations, you should then only have to take him for annual well visits.

Your dog's annual exams will be a lot like his first veterinary appointment. A veterinary technician will weigh your dog at the beginning of each visit, recording this information in his chart. The vet tech will then take you to an examination room and ask you a few routine questions, making note of anything that you should discuss when the vet joins you.

After looking over your German Shorthaired Pointer's chart, your veterinarian will most likely begin your dog's physical exam by checking his eyes, nose, and ears. All three should be clear of debris and discharge. The vet will then check his mouth and teeth. His gums should be pink (not red or white), and he shouldn't have any cuts or swelling on them. His teeth should be white and free of tartar. Using a stethoscope, your vet will listen to your GSP's heartbeat and his breathing. Your dog's heart rate should fall between 100 and 130 beats per minute, and his lungs should be free of congestion. Your vet will also check your dog's skin and coat, his abdomen, and all of his joints.

Puppy Love

TIMING YOUR GSP PUPPY'S VACCINATIONS

Your German Shorthaired Pointer will need to visit his veterinarian for vaccinations and booster shots more often during the first few months of his life than at any other time. It is important that he gets these important inoculations so that he is protected against deadly diseases such as distemper, parvovirus, and rabies. Many vets advise against administering too many shots during a single visit, however, especially if one of the shots is a combination vaccine. They suggest waiting at least a week or two between vaccinations to reduce the amount of stress on the animal's system. You may worry that multiple trips to the vet will be expensive, but many practices will waive the cost of the office visit on the subsequent appointments if you wish to spread out your puppy's vaccinations. Many pet supply stores also sponsor low-cost vaccination clinics as a means of helping owners better afford to keep their pets in good health.

One of the biggest mistakes you can make is skipping your dog's annual exam. Even if your dog appears healthy, your vet may pick up on something that you have missed during this routine visit. The prognosis for nearly every affliction is better when the problem is detected early.

You may also have to make an occasional appointment for your dog to see your vet between his routine checkups. Be sure to contact your vet if you notice any changes in your dog's body or behavior. Perhaps your dog is gaining weight without increasing his caloric intake, or maybe his appetite has waned. However minor they may seem, these changes can be a signal of a serious problem, such as hypothyroidism or Addison's disease. Remember, you know

your dog better than anyone else does. If something just doesn't feel right, it may be worth mentioning.

Vaccinations

Your breeder will have already begun your German Shorthaired Pointer's vaccination process by the time you take him home, but a puppy cannot receive the rabies vaccination until he is at least 12 weeks old. Other vaccinations, such as distemper and parvovirus, will require booster shots (repeated doses that ensure effectiveness), so you will be seeing your dog's vet frequently during the first few months.

The most routine procedures performed by veterinarians, vaccinations are a dog's best defense against many deadly diseases. Still, vaccinations are a controversial topic within the dog community—even veterinarians themselves occasionally disagree about which vaccines are safe and how often they should be administered. The dangers of overvaccinating dogs are subjects of constant research, and the findings can sometimes be rather confusing. Just as parents are educating themselves more about the vaccines offered to their infants and toddlers, pet owners are also becoming better informed about the benefits and liabilities of conventional vaccination schedules.

A vaccination essentially stimulates your dog's immune system to protect itself from disease. When a vaccine is injected into your GSP's body, it is instantly

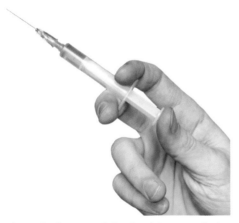

A vaccination essentially stimulates your dog's immune system to protect itself from disease.

recognized as a foreign agent. Antibodies are then produced to destroy it, setting an important precedent. The next time your dog's body is confronted with the same intruder, it will recognize the agent and respond even more quickly than the first time. Mimicking the body's own talent for creating immunity, vaccinations generally prevent a dog from falling victim to particular illnesses.

Some immunologists and veterinarians point out that problems can appear, though, when an animal is given too many different vaccines together or unnecessary repeated doses annually. Many experts insist that not only does immunity resulting from vaccinations last significantly longer than once believed, but also that continual boosters can actually weaken a dog's immune system, making the animal more vulnerable to such serious problems as acute allergies, epilepsy, and certain autoimmune diseases.

One option is to ask your veterinarian to administer only one vaccine at a time over several days, but availability of noncombination vaccinations might be a challenge. Also, many vets argue that the first shot creates a blocking effect, causing the dog's body to reject any other vaccines administered later.

Although both sides of the debate present convincing evidence supporting their theories on vaccinations, presently this issue is mostly a judgment call for owners. Skipping the vaccination process altogether, however, is not the answer. Dogs need vaccinations for such deadly diseases as distemper, parvovirus, and rabies. Because the law requires the rabies vaccination, you must conform to your state's timetable. Other vaccines and their frequency are a matter of education, circumstance, and preference. You should discuss these vaccines with your veterinarian and select a schedule of which you both approve.

Breed-Specific Illnesses

The German Shorthaired Pointer is generally a very healthy dog breed. Of course, every breed has at least some health problems to which it is prone, and the GSP is no exception. Fortunately, most of the illnesses your dog may develop are manageable.

Epilepsy

A condition of the central nervous system, epilepsy causes an animal to experience seizures at unexpected times. If your dog has epilepsy, he may seize once or twice every few months or once or twice every year. He may even seize only once every few years. The more often your dog's seizures occur, the more likely he will need to take an anticonvulsant medication to help control this condition.

During a seizure, a dog may shake, drool, and lose control of his bladder

The German Shorthaired Pointer is generally a very healthy dog breed.

or bowels. He may also experience a temporary paralysis or paddle his front legs as if he were swimming. One of my own dogs has epilepsy, and I can tell you firsthand that witnessing a seizure can be one of the most difficult things you will ever experience as a pet owner. As upsetting as it may be for you, though, your dog probably has very little awareness of what is happening during a seizure. He may not even recognize you during an episode. For this reason it is vital that you keep your face away from your dog's mouth, as he may bite you unintentionally.

If your dog experiences a seizure, call his veterinarian right away. The seizure itself will be long over before you can

SPAYING AND NEUTERING

The first vet visit is an excellent time to make plans to have your German Shorthaired Pointer spayed or neutered. Most dogs are ready for this routine surgery by the time they are just a few months old, but many owners wait until their dogs are at least a year old. In addition to helping control the unwanted pet population, owners who get a jump on this important step may be lengthening their dogs' lives. Many studies indicate that dogs who are sterilized early (before they reach puberty) have considerably lower risks for numerous types of cancer, the number-one killer of dogs today.

get your dog to the hospital, but it is important that your vet examine your pet to rule out an underlying cause of the problem. If your dog shows no sign of another illness, the diagnosis will be idiopathic epilsepy, which means that the cause is unknown.

Just as the frequency of your dog's seizures will help the vet decide whether medication is necessary, the intensity and length of the seizures will also play a role in this process. Dogs who experience infrequent petit mal (mild) seizures that last only a minute or two may not need any medication at all. Get your dog to an emergency clinic immediately, though, if he loses consciousness during a seizure or if the episode lasts longer than five minutes—both signs of a grand mal seizure (the most intense variety). Even if the seizure is over by the time you arrive, be sure to tell the vet if either of these situations occurs.

The most important thing to remember is not to panic. Your dog needs you to remain as calm as possible. As you learn more about how to care for your dog during one of these episodes, dealing with them does get easier.

Hermaphroditism

Hermaphroditism is a condition that causes both male and female reproductive organs to be present in the same animal. Although hermaphroditism is very rare in dogs, it is more common in German Shorthaired Pointers than in other breeds for some reason. On the outside, a dog may appear to be female, for example, but the animal's internal organs may include male organs such as testes. In many cases, a hermaphroditic pup will have an ovary on one side and a testicle on the other. Some have both a vulva and two testicles. A few will even have a gland that is both female and male, called an ovotestis.

If you notice that your dog's genitalia look unusual in any way—a bulging in the area of the vulva of your female dog, for instance—schedule an appointment with your vet, who will want to rule out the presence of a tumor. Most often, hermaphroditism is accompanied with infertility, but most vets recommend that an owner of a canine hermaphrodite have the pet sterilized to prevent complications that could result from an unplanned pregnancy.

Although hermaphroditism may seem like something straight out of the supermarket tabloids, do not be alarmed if your vet tells you that your German Shorthaired Pointer suffers from this problem. In most cases it causes no long-term effects on the animal, especially once the reproductive organs have been removed. Your dog is not a monster or a freak. Your pet simply experienced a genetic anomaly during gestational development.

Hip Dysplasia

Hip dysplasia is a common orthopedic problem in many dog breeds, including the German Shorthaired Pointer. It occurs when the hip socket doesn't fit together properly and causes lameness. Sometimes the problem is genetic, but it can also be caused by excessive exercise or an injury during the first years of a dog's life.

Because the problem is common in GSPs, be sure to confirm that both of your dog's parents have been cleared for the condition by the Orthopedic Foundation of America (OFA). Although clearances do not guarantee that your dog won't suffer from hip dysplasia, testing the parents is the first step in lessening a puppy's chances for developing the problem. Abstaining from rigorous exercise, like jogging or agility, while your dog is less than a year old is another way to prevent him from suffering from hip dysplasia. Even some dogs who are predisposed to dysplasia won't develop the condition if their owners play it safe when it comes to exercise.

If you notice your German Shorthaired Pointer limping, take him to his vet for a checkup immediately. An X-ray should provide a quick diagnosis if the problem is indeed hip dysplasia. Surgery for hip

If your dog seems unusually lethargic, take him to the veterinarian.

dysplasia includes replacing the hip with an artificial joint, but this may not be necessary if your dog's case is mild. If your dog is overweight, begin by placing him on a diet. In many cases, just shedding those excess pounds (kg) is enough to lessen the pain and discomfort by removing the amount of pressure on the animal's hips.

Ask your vet whether you can give your GSP an anti-inflammatory medication like aspirin to ease his pain. Your vet may be able to prescribe something stronger if necessary. When your dog is hurting, his exercise must be limited, but at other times movement can actually help. Just be sure that you don't let your dog overdo it. It is especially important that you do not allow your dog's muscles to atrophy, or shrink, as this can exacerbate the problem of dysplasia. Discourage your dog from jumping during exercise, however, as this behavior can aggravate the problem with his joints more than anything else. One of the best ways to ward off pain is by giving your dog his pain medication just prior to exercising.

Like people, dogs tend to shift their weight when a certain part of the body hurts. Although doing this may help them maintain their balance, it can lead to spinal problems due to improper alignment. For this reason, chiropractic care may also be useful. Dogs typically develop arthritis as a result of hip dysplasia.

Gastric Dilatation-Volvulus (GDV)

Many larger dog breeds, especially those with deep chests, are prone to a condition called gastric dilatation-volvulus (GDV). It is also sometimes referred to as bloat or torsion. GDV causes a dog's stomach to roll, twist, or even flip over. When this happens, the openings leading in and out of the stomach can become blocked and prevent the dog from belching or vomiting. It can also cut off blood supply to the stomach, inducing shock.

GDV is considered a medical emergency. If you notice your German Shorthaired Pointer trying to vomit to no avail, get him to the nearest veterinary hospital immediately. Surgery

can save a dog's life if the problem is identified quickly.

Eating or drinking too quickly can cause GDV. Other factors that may increase a dog's chances of suffering from this scary condition include eating a single large meal a day (feed your GSP at least two smaller meals instead), eating from a raised food bowl, and exercising too soon after eating. If your dog seems to gulp down his food no matter how much he has, opt to hand feed him instead as a means of slowing him down.

Lymphedema

Another condition to which German Shorthaired Pointers are prone is lymphedema. When a dog suffers from this problem, a lymphatic obstruction causes his body to retain fluid in a particular area, typically one of the legs. The leg then swells from the added fluid, making it feel very heavy. Movement and standing become difficult, and the dog usually experiences extreme fatigue. The affected area is at an increased risk for infection, as well as slower healing in the event of an injury. Swollen skin is considerably more prone to bacterial growth.

Most often lymphedema affects a dog's rear legs, although it can affect the front legs, ears, tail, or even the abdomen. Fluid retention usually starts around the feet and moves upward toward the body. Unfortunately, there is no cure for lymphedema. The only thing your vet can do is help you manage and reduce the intensity of the symptoms. Treatment may include bandaging the affected area, performing warm-water massages, and giving the dog antibiotics to fight infection and anti-inflammatory medications to reduce swelling.

General Illnesses

In addition to the ailments to which the German Shorthaired Pointer is prone, there are also a number of afflictions that commonly affect members of the canine community as a whole.

Allergies

When people suffer from allergies, they tend to sneeze or get watery eyes. They may even break out in hives or swell up like balloons. Dogs, on the other hand, tend to itch when they encounter an allergen. Most canine allergies are the result of something the dog has eaten. Common canine food allergens include beef, chicken, corn, and wheat, but your German Shorthaired Pointer can be allergic to absolutely anything—or even more than one thing. I once had a dog who was allergic to both potatoes and tomatoes.

The most obvious sign of a canine allergy is severe scratching. If your dog won't stop scratching, first check him for fleas. If you find none and he continues to itch and scratch, consider what you are feeding him. Because most dogs eat the same food every single day, they can develop an intolerance to a particular food over time. Your GSP puppy may have been able to eat beef, for example, without any obvious problems, but as an adult his adult body may be much less able to tolerate it.

Sometimes switching your dog from a food with one protein source to a food with a different one is enough to solve the problem. If you are feeding your pet a particular brand of food that you are happy with, there is no need to change to another. Instead try another formula from that company. Rather than a food made from beef, for instance, try feeding him one made from fish or venison. Even lamb, a meat that was once known as a virtual panacea for dogs with food allergies or intolerances, can be an allergen—especially if your dog has been eating it for a long time. Novel protein sources, those that most dogs and their genetic lines have not been exposed to in excess, are in fact your best choices when trying to find a hypoallergenic food for your pet.

Elimination diets can also be a useful tool in identifying a food allergen. If you cook for your German Shorthaired Pointer, remove one ingredient at a time from his diet, observing any changes that occur during his time without that specific food. If you notice no change when you remove beef, try removing chicken, and so on. Wait at least a week or two before judging the likelihood of each potential food allergen.

If the scratching persists, talk to your vet, who may suggest allergy testing as a means of identifying the offending allergen or allergens. A friend of mine found out that her dog was allergic to several different foods this way. The testing helped her avoid exposing her pet to many things she otherwise would have had to discover the hard way.

Some vets encourage dog owners to change pet foods every so often as a means of preventing food allergies from setting in. This can also be a great way of keeping variety in your dog's diet. If you go this route, just be sure to always choose a high-quality food for your GSP. Also, each time you make a change, introduce the new food gradually to avoid stomach upset. Mix the new food with the old food at a ratio of 25 to 75 percent the first week. The second week increase the amount of the new food to 50 percent, and the third week give your pet 75 percent of the new fare. By the end of a month's time, he should be completely transitioned to his new grub.

Arthritis

As your German Shorthaired Pointer gets older, he may develop a soreness in his

YOUR GSP'S FIRST-AID KIT

The following items should always be kept on hand in the event of a medical emergency:

- antibiotic ointment
- canine first-aid manual
- children's diphenhydramine (antihistamine)
- cotton swabs
- emergency phone numbers (including poison control, emergency veterinarian, and your dog's regular vet)
- hydrogen peroxide
- instant ice pack
- ipecac syrup

- liquid bandages
- nonstick gauze pads, gauze, and tape
- oral syringe or eyedropper
- rectal thermometer
- saline solution
- scissors
- styptic powder or pencil
- tweezers
- any other item your veterinarian recommends keeping on hand

Keep an eye on expiration dates, and replace any items that have passed the "best by" date printed on their packages.

joints called arthritis. The most noticeable sign of arthritis is painful movement. A dog suffering from arthritis may have a hard time standing up, climbing stairs, or walking for long periods. Pain is typically worse in the morning, but rain or cold weather can also exacerbate the problem.

If you suspect your GSP has arthritis, schedule an exam with your veterinarian. Once the problem has been diagnosed, your vet can help you create a plan of action to ease your dog's pain. There is no cure for arthritis, but the condition can be managed. Pain medications can offer patients relief. Many owners have also witnessed marked improvement after giving their dogs dietary supplements containing glucosamine, chondroitin, and methylsulfonylmethane (MSM). Talk to your vet about the best combinations and doses for your German Shorthaired Pointer based on his weight and age.

Making changes to your dog's environment can also ease the pain of arthritis. If your dog sleeps in a crate, make sure that it is positioned away from any drafts from doors or windows. Also, check the liner. Over time a padded liner can go from thick and luxurious to thin and threadbare.

The orthopedic foam that is so popular for mattresses made for people is also available in many pet products. It is an excellent material for both crate liners and dog beds.

If your GSP sleeps with you at night, jumping on and off your bed may be aggravating his pain. Special steps made specifically for dogs to access furniture more easily are now available in many pet supply stores. It may take you a short time to teach your dog to use his staircase faithfully, but it can be done. And many owners prefer training their dogs to use the steps to crating their pets for the first time as seniors.

Anything that makes your dog more comfortable can help make the arthritis take less of a toll. Even if your dog sleeps with you, consider placing a dog bed somewhere else in your home where he spends a great deal of time. An arthritic dog may enjoy sleeping on a tile floor because it can feel good on his belly, but doing so can be bad for his joints. A safety gate can help you block your dog's access to areas in which he shouldn't be spending large amounts of time.

Cancer

At one time just the word "cancer" was enough to instill fear in any dog owner. Although it still has a scary connotation, cancer is no longer the automatic death sentence that it was just a decade ago.

Early detection and veterinary technology both help keep problems like mast cell tumors (one of the most common forms of canine cancer) from taking the lives of our precious pets.

Examine your dog closely whenever patting him or grooming him. If you notice any unusual lumps or bumps, schedule a vet appointment to have them checked. A fine-needle aspiration is a quick way to perform a biopsy of almost any growth you find on the surface of your dog's skin. Many dogs suffer from benign fatty tumors as they age. This is most likely what your dog's growth is. If the tumor is malignant, however, discovering it early will make your vet's chances of removing it successfully much greater.

Other common types of canine cancer include brain tumors (characterized by seizures or extreme behavioral changes), mammary carcinomas (canine breast cancer), and melanomas (skin cancer). Radiation, surgery, or a combination of these treatment options often produces impressively positive outcomes in these cases. Again, the most important thing is early detection.

Complementary Therapies

Complementary medicine, sometimes called alternative medicine, has become an increasingly popular group of modalities in the veterinary community.

An ancient form of Chinese medicine, acupuncture also can be used on animals.

More and more owners want holistic treatment options for their pets, and vets everywhere are rising to this challenge. Many veterinarians now offer ancient healing approaches like acupuncture and homeopathy, as well as more contemporary techniques, such as chiropractic care and physical therapy, in conjunction with conventional veterinary medicine.

Acupuncture

The word "holistic" means "whole." Holistic treatments focus on the patient as a whole being. Before performing acupuncture on a dog with urinary incontinence, the acupuncturist will talk to you about the surrounding circumstances to get a clear picture of the problem. Sometimes the details help determine which of the more than 300 acupuncture points the vet needs to stimulate to achieve the desired results.

An ancient form of Chinese medicine, acupuncture can be traced back at least 2,500 years. By inserting tiny needles into specific points on the body, an acupuncturist aims to release healing energy within the body, called *qi* (pronounced CHEE). While many people have a hard time getting beyond the mechanics of this modality, proponents of acupuncture insist that, much like human patients, animals feel absolutely no pain from the thread-like needles.

The American Veterinary Medical Association (AVMA) acknowledges acupuncture as "an integral part of veterinary medicine." This is no small endorsement. Perhaps better than anything else, the AVMA's approval shows pet owners that complementary techniques are not as off the wall as they may initially seem. Whether used alone or in conjunction with conventional methods, complementary modalities can offer impressive success. To find a canine acupuncturist in your area, contact the American Academy of Veterinary Acupuncture (AAVA) at www.aava.org.

Homeopathy

Like acupuncture, homeopathy stimulates the body to heal itself. Based on a very similar principle as the vaccination process, homeopathic medicine works by implementing infinitesimal doses of the substances that actually cause the disease a caregiver wishes to cure. While the amounts of the substances used in homeopathy are far removed from that of a vaccination, the premise of homeopathy is that the more these substances are diluted, the more powerful the effect on the patient will be.

When treated with homeopathic medicine, a dog may actually exhibit an intensification of symptoms before improvement begins. A German Shorthaired Pointer with a fever, for example, may at first experience an even higher temperature. The ultimate goal, however, is a complete removal of all symptoms by creating a natural resistance to the illness.

Homeopathy is not something with which dog owners should experiment. Although it may be tempting to apply any knowledge you may already have in this area to your dog's current condition, it is always best to seek the advice of a trained professional, preferably a licensed veterinarian who is also trained in this particular branch of complementary medicine. Because the process involves such precise dosages, a high level of vigilance in treatment is mandatory.

Physical Therapy

The field of physical therapy is one of the most expanding professions within the human medical care community. People rely on this productive resource for help with all kinds of physical issues, ranging from hip dysplasia to strokes. It makes sense that canine patients suffering from these same problems can benefit from the canine version of this effective treatment. With the aid of such technological tools as ultrasound and electrical stimulation, canine physical therapists often start

Check It Out

HEALTH CARE CHECKLIST

✓ Take your time selecting a veterinarian for your dog. This important person will be your foremost partner in your dog's care.

✓ Take your dog to his vet for annual checkups. Consider increasing the frequency of these routine exams to twice a year once your dog reaches eight years of age.

✓ Vaccinate your dog against the most deadly diseases, but consider having titers taken before revaccinating, as many vaccines last much longer than originally thought.

✓ Always be on the lookout for changes in your dog's body and temperament, as these can be signs of illness. Remember, early detection is your best weapon in fighting any disease.

✓ Be open to alternative therapies like acupuncture and physical therapy. The best caregivers are licensed veterinarians who have been trained in these complementary modalities.

where conventional veterinarians leave off—after surgical procedures, during the healing of an injury to increase range of motion and overall strength, and even as a means of reducing pain and stiffness associated with a variety of chronic conditions. Canine physical therapists also utilize more traditional modalities such as massage, hydrotherapy (water), and therapeutic exercise. The exact combination of treatments depends on your dog's individual needs.

Any veterinarian can legally perform canine physical therapy, but it is important to note that very few vets receive training in this area as part of their formal education. Ideally, I recommend looking for a veterinarian who is also a licensed physical therapist for human patients. If you have trouble finding one of these dually trained individuals, however, expand your search to find both a veterinarian and physical therapist who are willing to work together for the betterment of your German Shorthaired Pointer's health.

Senior GSPs

As your German Shorthaired Pointer starts to get older—around the age of eight—his body will begin showing signs of his age. You may notice that his

GSPs become seniors at about eight years of age.

metabolism has slowed somewhat or that his coat now has a few gray hairs. He may sleep more or take a little extra time climbing the stairs. Some dogs develop warts or fatty tumors on various parts of their body as they age. Most of these growths will be benign, but each and every one should be checked by your vet.

Increase Frequency of Vet Visits

Healthy dogs tolerate the aging process much better than sick ones do, so I suggest increasing the frequency of your GSP's routine exams to once every six months as he enters his senior years. If a problem arises, your chances of discovering it early will be much better this way. Early diagnosis usually translates to a more positive prognosis.

Keep His Mind and Body Fit

Another excellent way to keep your dog healthy is by keeping both his mind and body fit. Make exercise a priority, even as your pet gets older, and continue to teach your older dog new tricks to keep his mind sharp. He may not be able to run as fast as he did when he was younger, but you can adjust your routine to match his energy level and abilities.

Adjust His Diet

Another thing you should consider adjusting is your aging German Shorthaired Pointer's diet. Older dogs tend to gain weight more quickly than younger ones, so you may need to feed your older GSP a bit less food. Additionally, you may want to switch your older pet to a dog food formula made specifically for senior dogs. Many of these formulas have lower protein levels and include supplements like glucosamine and chondroitin, which are known to help conditions like arthritis. Because older dogs sometimes lose interest in food, you may need to employ a few tricks to keep your dog's appetite where it should be. Serving wet food or adding a bit of water to your dog's kibble and heating his dinner are great ways to release the food's aroma and therefore make the food more appealing to your pet. You may even consider supplementing your dog's dry food with home-cooked fare.

Schedule a Professional Teeth Cleaning

If your dog has a lot of tartar on his teeth, this may also be a smart time to schedule a professional cleaning, also called a scaling. Your dog must be fit and healthy to have this done because he must be anesthetized for the procedure. If you have been remiss about brushing his teeth, though, it will be in your dog's best interest to have his teeth cleaned. Periodontal disease can make eating uncomfortable for your pet. It can also lead to many additional health problems in older pets—including a dangerous type of heart disease called bacterial endocarditis. Your vet will also extract any infected or loose teeth while your GSP is under the anesthesia.

Ease His Aches and Pains

If your dog does have any ailments like arthritis (one of the most common conditions of old age), you can help ease some of his aches and pains by providing him with a bed made from orthopedic foam. Keeping him warm will also help him feel more comfortable. A reasonable amount of exercise can help your dog maintain flexibility and mobility. Watch him closely for signs that he's had enough, but when he wants to play, by all means indulge him. He may be looking his age on the outside, but on the inside he is still the same playful pup he was when you first brought him home.

Resources

Associations and Organizations

Breed Clubs

American Kennel Club (AKC)
5580 Centerview Drive
Raleigh, NC 27606
Telephone: (919) 233-9767
Fax: (919) 233-3627
E-Mail: info@akc.org
www.akc.org

Canadian Kennel Club (CKC)
89 Skyway Avenue, Suite 100
Etobicoke, Ontario M9W 6R4
Telephone: (416) 675-5511
Fax: (416) 675-6506
E-Mail: information@ckc.ca
www.ckc.ca

Federation Cynologique Internationale (FCI)
Secretariat General de la FCI
Place Albert 1er, 13
B – 6530 Thuin
Belgique
www.fci.be

German Shorthaired Pointer Club of America (GSPCA)
www.gspca.org

German Shorthaired Pointer Club of Cananda (GSPCC)
www.gspcanada.com

The German Shorthaired Pointer Club
www.gsp.org.uk

The Kennel Club
1 Clarges Street
London
W1J 8AB
Telephone: 0870 606 6750
Fax: 0207 518 1058
www.the-kennel-club.org.uk

United Kennel Club (UKC)
100 E. Kilgore Road
Kalamazoo, MI 49002-5584
Telephone: (269) 343-9020
Fax: (269) 343-7037
E-Mail: pbickell@ukcdogs.com
www.ukcdogs.com

Pet Sitters

National Association of Professional Pet Sitters
15000 Commerce Parkway, Suite C
Mt. Laurel, NJ 08054
Telephone: (856) 439-0324
Fax: (856) 439-0525
E-Mail: napps@ahint.com
www.petsitters.org

Pet Sitters International
201 East King Street
King, NC 27021-9161
Telephone: (336) 983-9222
Fax: (336) 983-5266
E-Mail: info@petsit.com
www.petsit.com

Rescue Organizations and Animal Welfare Groups

American Humane Association (AHA)
63 Inverness Drive East
Englewood, CO 80112
Telephone: (303) 792-9900
Fax: 792-5533
www.americanhumane.org

American Society for the Prevention of Cruelty to Animals (ASPCA)
424 E. 92nd Street
New York, NY 10128-6804
Telephone: (212) 876-7700
www.aspca.org

The Humane Society of the United States (HSUS)
2100 L Street, NW
Washington, DC 20037
Telephone: (202) 452-1100
www.hsus.org

Royal Society for the Prevention of Cruelty to Animals (RSPCA)
RSPCA Enquiries Service
Wilberforce Way, Southwater,
Horsham, West Sussex RH13 9RS
United Kingdom
Telephone: 0870 3335 999
Fax: 0870 7530 284
www.rspca.org.uk

Sports
International Agility Link (IAL)
Global Administrator: Steve Drinkwater
E-Mail: yunde@powerup.au
www.agilityclick.com/~ial

The World Canine Freestyle Organization, Inc.
P.O. Box 350122
Brooklyn, NY 11235
Telephone: (718) 332-8336
Fax: (718) 646-2686
E-Mail: WCFODOGS@aol.com
www.worldcaninefreestyle.org

Therapy
Delta Society
875 124th Ave, NE, Suite 101
Bellevue, WA 98005
Telephone: (425) 679-5500
Fax: (425) 679-5539
E-Mail: info@DeltaSociety.org
www.deltasociety.org

Therapy Dogs Inc.
P.O. Box 20227
Cheyenne, WY 82003
Telephone: (877) 843-7364
Fax: (307) 638-2079
E-Mail: therapydogsinc@qwestoffice.net
www.therapydogs.com

Therapy Dogs International (TDI)
88 Bartley Road
Flanders, NJ 07836
Telephone: (973) 252-9800
Fax: (973) 252-7171
E-Mail: tdi@gti.net
www.tdi-dog.org

Training
Association of Pet Dog Trainers (APDT)
150 Executive Center Drive Box 35
Greenville, SC 29615
Telephone: (800) PET-DOGS
Fax: (864) 331-0767
E-Mail: information@apdt.com
www.apdt.com

International Association of Animal Behavior Consultants (IAABC)
565 Callery Road
Cranberry Township, PA 16066
E-Mail: info@iaabc.org
www.iaabc.org

National Association of Dog Obedience Instructors (NADOI)
PMB 369
729 Grapevine Hwy.
Hurst, TX 76054-2085
www.nadoi.org

Veterinary and Health Resources

Academy of Veterinary Homeopathy (AVH)
P.O. Box 9280
Wilmington, DE 19809
Telephone: (866) 652-1590
Fax: (866) 652-1590
www.theavh.org

American Academy of Veterinary Acupuncture (AAVA)
P.O. Box 1058
Glastonbury, CT 06033
Telephone: (860) 632-9911
Fax: (860) 659-8772
www.aava.org

American Animal Hospital Association (AAHA)
12575 W. Bayaud Ave.
Lakewood, CO 80228
Telephone: (303) 986-2800
Fax: (303) 986-1700
E-Mail: info@aahanet.org
www.aahanet.org/index.cfm

American College of Veterinary Internal Medicine (ACVIM)
1997 Wadsworth Blvd., Suite A
Lakewood, CO 80214-5293
Telephone: (800) 245-9081
Fax: (303) 231-0880
E-Mail: ACVIM@ACVIM.org
www.acvim.org

American College of Veterinary Ophthalmologists (ACVO)
P.O. Box 1311
Meridian, ID 83860
Telephone: (208) 466-7624
Fax: (208) 466-7693
E-Mail: office09@acvo.com
www.acvo.com

American Holistic Veterinary Medical Association (AHVMA)
2218 Old Emmorton Road
Bel Air, MD 21015
Telephone: (410) 569-0795
Fax: (410) 569-2346
E-Mail: office@ahvma.org
www.ahvma.org

American Veterinary Medical Association (AVMA)
1931 North Meacham Road, Suite 100
Schaumburg, IL 60173-4360
Telephone: (847) 925-8070
Fax: (847) 925-1329
E-Mail: avmainfo@avma.org
www.avma.org

ASPCA Animal Poison Control Center
Telephone: (888) 426-4435
www.aspca.org

British Veterinary Association (BVA)
7 Mansfield Street
London
W1G 9NQ
Telephone: 0207 636 6541
Fax: 0207 908 6349
E-Mail: bvahq@bva.co.uk
www.bva.co.uk

Canine Eye Registration Foundation (CERF)
VMDB/CERF
1717 Philo Rd
P O Box 3007
Urbana, IL 61803-3007
Telephone: (217) 693-4800
Fax: (217) 693-4801
E-Mail: CERF@vmbd.org
www.vmdb.org

Orthopedic Foundation for Animals (OFA)
2300 NE Nifong Blvd
Columbus, MO 65201-3856
Telephone: (573) 442-0418
Fax: (573) 875-5073
E-Mail: ofa@offa.org
www.offa.org

US Food and Drug Administration Center for Veterinary Medicine (CVM)
7519 Standish Place
HFV-12
Rockville, MD 20855-0001
Telephone: (240) 276-9300 or (888) INFO-FDA
http://www.fda.gov/cvm

Publications

Books

Anderson, Teoti. *The Super Simple Guide to Housetraining.* Neptune City: TFH Publications, 2004.

Anne, Jonna, with Mary Straus. *The Healthy Dog Cookbook: 50 Nutritious and Delicious Recipes Your Dog Will Love.* UK: Ivy Press Limited, 2008.

Dainty, Suellen. *50 Games to Play With Your Dog.* UK: Ivy Press Limited, 2007.

Morgan, Diane. *Good Dogkeeping.* Neptune City: TFH Publications, 2005.

Magazines

AKC Family Dog
American Kennel Club
260 Madison Avenue
New York, NY 10016
Telephone: (800) 490-5675
E-Mail: familydog@akc.org
www.akc.org/pubs/familydog

AKC Gazette
American Kennel Club
260 Madison Avenue
New York, NY 10016
Telephone: (800) 533-7323
E-Mail: gazette@akc.org
www.akc.org/pubs/gazette

Dog & Kennel
Pet Publishing, Inc.
7-L Dundas Circle
Greensboro, NC 27407
Telephone: (336) 292-4272
Fax: (336) 292-4272
E-Mail: info@petpublishing.com
www.dogandkennel.com

Dogs Monthly
Ascot House
High Street, Ascot,
Berkshire SL5 7JG
United Kingdom
Telephone: 0870 730 8433
Fax: 0870 730 8431
E-Mail: admin@rtc-associates.freeserve.co.uk
www.corsini.co.uk/dogsmonthly

Websites

Nylabone
www.nylabone.com

TFH Publications, Inc.
www.tfh.com

Index

Note: **Boldfaced** numbers indicate illustrations.

A

accidents, housetraining, 25, 75–76, 90–92
activities. *See* sports and activities
acupuncture, **129,** 129–130
aggression, 92, 94, 95
agility, 103–104
air travel, 26, 101–102, 110
allergies, 37, 39, 125–126
alternative medicine, 114, 115, 128–131, **129**
American Academy of Veterinary Acupuncture (AAVA), 130
American Kennel Club (AKC), 8, 9, 104–105, 106
American Veterinary Medical Association (AVMA), 130
animal welfare groups, 134–135
arthritis, 126–128, 133
Association of Pet Dog Trainers (APDT), 77
associations, 134–137

B

BARF diet, 46–47
barking, 84–87, **86,** 94
Barn Elms Show, 9
bathing, 54–57, 62
    supplies for, 29
    training for, 67
beds, 27–28, 127–128, 133
behaviorists, 92
behavior problems. *See* problem behaviors
belly band, 93
Best in Show titles, 7, 8, 9, 68
bison meat, 37
biting, 94, 95
bloat, 124–125
blow drying, 57
boarding services, 102–103
body block, 94–95
books, 137
booster shots, 117, 119
brain tumors, 128
breakaway collars, 21
breed, choosing right, 68
breed clubs, 8, 9, 134
breed standard, 9, 105, **105**

brushing, 52–53, 62
    pre-bath, 54
    supplies for, 28–29, **54**

C

calcium, 40
cancer, 122, 128
Canine Good Citizen program, 104–105, 111
canned food, **36,** 41, 43
carbohydrates, 36, 39
carrots, 42, **42**
carsickness, 101
Carter, Blaine, 12
car travel, 26, 100–101, 110
Casey, Len, 7
cats and GSP, 14
cedar shavings, 27–28
ceramic dishes, 24
chain leashes, 22
characteristics, 10–15
    checklist for, 15
    living situation and, 14–15
    physical, 6, 12–14
    temperament, 7, 13, 14
chewing, **87,** 87–88, 94
    drop it and *leave it* for, 89
    toys for, 25, **31,** 32, 61, 87–88
children and GSP, 70, 71
choke collars, 19–20
chondroitin, 127, 133
clicker training, 67–68, 78
coat, 13
coat care, 52–57, **54,** 62
collars, 18–21, **19**
color, coat, 6, 12
come command, 66–67, 79–80
commands, 66–67, 76–81
    come, 66–67, 79–80
    down, 80–81
    down-stay, 80, 81, 86, **86**
    drop it and *leave it,* 88, 89
    eliminating on, 76
    enough, 85
    heel, 81
    release, 79
    shake, 56, 57
    sit, **76,** 78–79
    sit-stay, 79, 93–94
    stay, 67, 79
    watch me, 76–78
commercial foods, **36, 41,** 41–44

companionability, 14, **14**
complementary therapies, 114, 115, 128–131, **129**
conformation, **105,** 105–107
    Best in Show titles in, 7, 8, 9, 68
    checklist for, 110
consistency in training, 85
cotton collars, 19
cotton leashes, 22
crate liner, 27, 127–128
crates, 24–27, **26**
    for arthritic dog, 127–128
    for travel, 100–102
crate training, 66, 69, 72–74

D

dairy products, 40, 46
dental care, 60–61, 62
    feeding and, 43, 44
    for seniors, 133
    supplies for, 28, 29
    toothbrushing in, 53, 60, **61**
dermatitis, plastic dish, 24
Detterich, Karen, 20
diet. *See* feeding
diet pills, 49
digging, 88, 90, **90,** 94
dirlotapide, 49
distemper vaccination, 119, 121
dog cake, 41
dog food rolls, 44
dogs, GSP and other, 14, **14, 70,** 71–72
dog showing. *See* conformation
down command, 80–81
down-stay command, 80, 81, 86, **86**
drop it command, 88, 89
dry food, 37, **41,** 41–42

E

ear care, 29, **58,** 58–59, 62
ears, 13
ectropion, 60
eggs, 46
elimination diets, 126
emergency care, 117, 127
endocarditis, bacterial, 60, 133
energy level, 12, 14, 15
England, GSP in, 8, 9
English Pointer, 7
environment, 14–15
epilepsy, 121–122

exercise, 15, 114. *See also* sports and activities
  hip dysplasia and, 124
  for obesity, 48–49
  for seniors, 132, 133
  toys for, 32
eye care, **59,** 60, 62
eyes, 13

F

fats, 36, 38
fatty tumors, 128, 132
feeding, 34–49, 114
  allergies related to, 37, 39, 125, 126
  changing foods for, 23, 40, 44, 126
  checklist for, 48
  commercial foods for, **36, 41,** 41–44
  free vs. scheduled, 47, **47**
  gastric dilatation-volvulus and, 124–125
  housetraining and, 75
  noncommercial foods for, **42,** 44–47, **45**
  nutrients for, 36–41
  obesity and, 47–49
  puppy, 40
  senior, 133
  supplements for, 39–41, 127, 133
  supplies for, 22–24, **23, 24**
feet, handling, 63
fences, 15
field trials, 108, **108,** 110
first-aid kit, 127
fish, 37, 40
flyball, 107
folic acid, 40
food allergies, 37, 39, 125, 126
food bowls, 22–24, **23, 24**
free feeding, 47, **47**
fruits, 39, 40, 42

G

gastric dilatation-volvulus (GDV), 124–125
gates, safety, 28, 73
gauze toothbrush, 29, 61
genitalia, abnormal, 122–123
German Bird Dog, 7
German Kennel Club, 7, 8
German Shorthaired Pointer Club of

America, 8
Germany, GSP in, 7–9
ginger, 101
glucosamine, 40–41, 127, 133
grains, 39
grooming, 50–63, 114
  checklist for, 62
  coat and skin care in, 52–57, **54**
  dental care in, 53, 60–61, **61**
  ear care in, **58,** 58–59
  eye care in, **59,** 60
  nail care in, 61–63, **63**
  puppy, 57
  supplies for, **28,** 28–29, 52
  training for, 52–53, 56, 57, 67
grooming mitt, 28, **28**

H

hand signals, 78–79
head harness, 20
health care, 114–121. *See also* illnesses; veterinarian
  annual visit for, 117–119
  for breed-specific illnesses, 121–125
  checklist for, 131
  complementary therapies in, 128–131
  finding vet for, **114,** 114–117
  first-aid kit for, 127
  for general illnesses, 125–128
  resources for, 136–137
  for seniors, 131–133
  spaying and neutering in, 122
  vaccinations in, 119–121, **120**
heart rate, 118
heartworm preventative, 99
heel command, 81
hermaphroditism, 122–123
hip dysplasia, 123–124
history of German Shorthaired Pointer, 4–9
  Best in Show titles in, 7
  in England and United States, 9
  in Germany, 7, 9
  timeline for, 8
holistic care, 114, 115, 128–131
home-cooked diet, 44, **45,** 45–46, 48
homeopathy, 130
hotels, pet-friendly, 102
house soiling, 90–93, 94
housetraining, 66, 74–76, **75**

crate for, 25, 72–73, 74
remedial, 91–92
hunting, 107, 108, **108,** 110
hunting dogs, 12, 68

I

identification, 21, **29,** 30–31, 102
illnesses. *See also* health care
  breed-specific, 121–125
  carsickness, 101
  dental, 60, 133
  ear, 58, 59
  eye, 60
  food-related, 37, 39, 46–47
  general, 125–128
  house soiling and, 92
  nutrition for, 40–41
  obesity and, 47–48
  plastic and, 24, 32–33
  signs of, 119, 131
  vaccine-related, 120
Internet resources, 102, 115, 137

J

jogging, 49
jumping up, 93–95

K

kibble, 37, **41,** 41–42
Klub Kurzhaar, 8, 9
Kurzhaar, 7

L

lamb, 37, 126
lead in tableware, 24
leashes
  types of, **21,** 21–22
  walking on, 73, 81
leather collars, 19, **19**
leather leashes, 22
leave it command, 88, 89
legs, 14
liver and liver roan colors, 6
living with GSP, **14,** 14–15
lodging, pet-friendly, 102
Lowe, Robert, 68
Lucas, Joy, 44
lymphedema, 125

M

magazines, 137
Maniet, Monique, 115
marking, 93

martingale collar, 20
mast cell tumors, 128
meat, 37, 39, 40
    home-cooked, 44
    raw, 46, 47
meat by-products, 36, 37–38
meat meal, 37
methylsulfonylmethane (MSM), 127
microchips, 30–31
minerals, 36, 39–41
Mitchell, Scott, 91
motion sickness, 101
muzzle, 13

N

nail care, 61–63, **63**
nail clippers, 28, 29, 62, 63, **63**
neutering, 93, 122
nipping, 95
noncommercial foods, **42,** 44–47, **45**
nutrients, 36–41, 48
Nylabone products, **15,** 32, **33, 49,**
    60, 61, **88, 137**
nylon collars, 19, 21
nylon leashes, 22

O

obedience
    basic, 15, 66–67, 76–81
    competitive, 108–109
    rally, 109–111
obesity, 38, 47–49
older dogs. *See* senior dogs
omega-3 fatty acids, 37
onions, 42
operant conditioning, 68
organizations, 134–137
Orthopedic Foundation of America
    (OFA), 123
ovotestis, 122

P

pain management, 124, 127, 133
parvovirus vaccination, 119, 121
paws, handling, 63
people
    companionability with, 14
    socialization to, 13, 69, 71, 95
periodontal disease, 60, 133
pets
    companionability with other,
      14, **14**
    hunting dogs as, 12, 68

socialization to other, 13, 69, **70,**
    71–72
pet sitters, 102, 134
pet supply stores, 18
phthalates, 32–33
physical characteristics, 6, 12–14, 15
physical therapy, 130–131
pinch collars, 20
plastic crates, 25, 26, **26**
plastic dishes, 24, **24**
plastic toys, 32–33
play, 69
positive training, **67,** 67–69, 77, 80
praise, 69
prescription diets, 40, 48, 49
preservatives, 43
problem behaviors, 82–95
    barking, 84–87, **86**
    checklist for, 94
    chewing, **87,** 87–88, 89
    digging, 88, 90, **90**
    house soiling, 90–93
    jumping up, 93–95
    nipping and biting, 95
    professional help for, 92
    puppies and, 85
    stumbling block for, 91
professional help, 77, 92, 95
prong collars, 20
proteins, 36–38
publications, 137
puppies
    agility for, 103
    beds for, 28
    "birdiness" test for, 108
    Canine Good Citizen and, 105
    chewing by, 25, **31, 87,** 87–88
    collars for, 18–19
    crate size for, 27
    feeding, 40, 47, **47**
    grooming, 52–53, 57, 62
    home prep for, 20, 87
    housetraining, 74
    leash training, 73
    nipping by, 95
    problem behaviors in, 85
    socialization of, 13
    training sessions for, 68
    vaccinations for, 119
puppy mills, 72–73
PVC (polyvinyl chloride), 33

Q

qi, 129
quick of nail, 63

R

rabies vaccination, 119, 121
rally obedience, 109–111
raw diet, 46–47, 48
release command, 79
rescue organizations, 134–135
resources, 134–137
Responsible Dog Owner Pledge, 104
retractable leashes, 22
rewards, training, 69
running, 49
Rutar, Charlene, 107

S

safety, 66–67, 89, 98
safety gates, 28, 73
salt, 45
sandbox, 88, 90
schedules
    elimination, 74, 91
    feeding, 40, 47, **47**
    vaccination, 119, 120–121
Schwarzenegger, Arnold, 33
seat belt, canine, 100–101
seizures, 121–122
semi-moist food, 43–44
senior dogs, **132**
    arthritis in, 126–128
    feeding, 43
    health care for, 131–133
separation anxiety, 92
shake command, 56, 57
shampoo, 29, 56
shedding, 28–29, 52, 53
sit command, **76,** 78–79
sit-stay command, 79, 93–94
size, body, 13
skin care, 52–57, **54**
slip collars, 19–20
Smith, Elaine, 111
socialization, 66, 69–72
    to other animals, **70,** 71–72
    to people, 71
    for problem behaviors, 86, 95
    puppy, 13
soft-sided crates, 25
Sova, Paul, 53
Spanish Pointer, 7
spaying, 122

Sporting Group, 105
sports and activities, 96–111, **99**
　agility, 103–104
　Canine Good Citizen, 104–105
　checklist for, 110
　conformation, 7, 8, 9, 68, **105,**
　　105–107
　flyball, 107
　hunting and field trials, 107, 108,
　　108
　obedience, 108–109
　for obesity, 49
　rally obedience, 109–111
　resources for, 135
　safety for, 98
　therapy work, 111
　traveling, 98–103
stainless steel bowls, **23,** 23–24
staircase, canine, 128
stay command, 67, 79
supplements, 39–41, 127, 133
supplies, 16–33
　beds, 27–28
　checklist for, 32
　collars, 18–21, **19**
　crates, 24–27, **26**
　first-aid, 127
　food and water bowls, 22–24,
　　23, 24
　grooming, **28,** 28–29, 52
　identification, **29,** 30–31
　leashes, **21,** 21–22
　safety gates, 28
　toys, 25, **31,** 31–33
　travel, 99–100

T

tags, ID, 21, **29,** 30
tail, 14
tattoos, 31
tearstains, 60
teething, 25, 87
temperament, 7, 13, 14
Therapy Dogs International (TDI),
　110, 111
therapy work, 110, 111, 135
toothbrush and toothpaste, 28, 29,
　61, **61**. *See also* dental care
torsion, gastric, 124–125
toys, 31–33
　chew, 25, **31,** 32, 61, 87–88
　labels on, 33
　for sandbox, 90
　training with, 69

vinyl, 32–33
trainability, 15
trainers, 77, 92
training, 64–81. *See also* problem
　behaviors
　advanced obedience, 108–109
　basic commands for, 76–81
　breed choice for, 68
　checklist for, 80
　consistency in, 85
　crate, 72–74
　finding trainer for, 77
　for grooming, 52–53, 56, 57
　housetraining, 74–76, **75,** 91–92
　leash, 73
　positive, **67,** 67–69, 77, 80
　reasons for, 66–67
　resources for, 135
　socialization, 13, 69–72, **70,** 86, 95
traveling, 98–103
　by air, 101–102
　by car, 100–101
　checklist for, 110
　crates for, 26
　lodging for, 102
　supplies for, 99–100
　vet checkup before, 99
　without dog, 102–103
treats, training, 69, 70
tumors, benign, 128, 132
turkey, 37

U

undercoat, 53
United States, GSP in, 8, 9

V

vaccinations, 119–121, **120,** 131
　booster, 117
　pre-travel, 99
　puppy, 119
vegetables
　adding to diet, 42, **42,** 44, 46
　nutrients in, 39, 40
veterinarian. *See also* health care
　conventional vs. holistic, 115
　finding, **114,** 114–117, 131
　physical therapy by, 131
veterinary care
　annual, 117–119
　dental, 53, 60
　for house soiling, 92
　initial, 117
　for obesity, 49

　pre-travel, 99
　resources for, 136–137
　for seniors, 132
Veterinary Holistic Care, 115
vinyl toys, 32–33
visual cues, 78–79, 80, 81
vitamins, 36, 38, 39–41, 48

W

walking on leash, 73, 81
watch me command, 76–78
water, 37, 75, 98
water bowls, 22–24, **23, 24**
websites, 102, 115, 137
weight, 13, 38, 47–49
Westminster Best in Show titles, 7,
　8, 9, 68
wire crates, 25, 27
wolves, 39, 46
wooden crates, 25

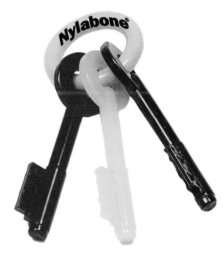

Photo Credits

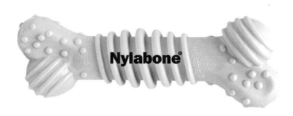

Dedication

To Bill Culmer—in this mad, mad, mad, mad world we live in, I am proud to call you my friend.

Acknowledgments

I would like to thank the following breeders for taking the time to speak with me about their experiences with German Shorthaired Pointers:

- Carol Chadwick, Northwood Mountain Kennels, Elk Grove, California
- Karen Detterich, Paladen Kennels, Southern California
- Charlene Rutar, White River Shorthairs, Noblesville, Indiana

And a special thank you to Judy Moore, a skilled trainer who has given me an even deeper insight into the canine heart and mind.

About the Author

Tammy Gagne is a freelance writer who specializes in the health and behavior of companion animals. In addition to writing dozens of articles for several national pet care magazines, she has authored more than 30 books about animals for both adults and children. Her breed guide, *The Cocker Spaniel*, was nominated for a Dog Writers Association of America (DWAA) award in 2006. She resides in northern New England with her husband, son, dogs, and parrots.

Nylabone®

3 1143 00931 5897

JOIN NOW
Club Nylabone
www.nylabone.com
Coupons!
Articles!
Exciting
Features!

He **Plays** Hard.
He **Chews** Hard.

He's a **Nylabone®** Dog!

Your #1 choice for healthy chews & treats.